STUDIES IN ENGLISH LITERATURE No. 35

General Editor

David Daiches

Dean of the School of English and American Studies,
University of Sussex

To My Parents

SHAKESPEARE:
A MIDSUMMER NIGHT'S DREAM

by
STEPHEN FENDER

Lecturer in English Literature,
The University, Edinburgh

EDWARD ARNOLD (PUBLISHERS) LTD
41 Maddox Street, London, W.1

Printed in Great Britain by
The Camelot Press Ltd., London and Southampton

General Preface

It has become increasingly clear in recent years that what both the advanced sixth-former and the university student need most by way of help in their literary studies are close critical analyses and evaluations of individual works. Generalisations about periods or authors, general chat about the Augustan Age or the Romantic Movement, have their uses; but often they provide merely the illusion of knowledge and understanding of literature. All too often students come up to the university under the impression that what is required of them in their English literature courses is the referring of particular works to the appropriate generalisations about the writer or his period. Without taking up the anti-historical position of some of the American 'New Critics', we can nevertheless recognise the need for critical studies that concentrate on the work of literary art rather than on its historical background or cultural movement.

The present series is therefore designed to provide studies of individual plays, novels and groups of poems and essays, which are known to be widely studied in sixth forms and in universities. The emphasis is on clarification and evaluation; biographical and historical facts, while they may of course be referred to as helpful to an understanding of particular elements in a writer's work, will be subordinated to critical discussion. What kind of work is this? What exactly goes on here? How good is this work, and why? These are the questions which each writer will try to answer.

DAVID DAICHES

Acknowledgements

I am especially grateful to the following people for helping me with this book: Eluned Brown, John Ellis, Buffy Fender, Professor Harold Jenkins, Professor Frank Kermode, and Professor Moelwyn Merchant. I should also like to express a more general debt to the first- and final-year students with whom I have studied *A Midsummer Night's Dream* at Edinburgh.

Contents

We cannot go back to that.
The squirming facts exceed the squamous mind,
If one may say so.

WALLACE STEVENS

1. Introduction: Play or Opera?

The scene is a wood outside Athens. Four exhausted adolescent lovers —their clothes in some disarray—lie asleep in the dirt. Enter Theseus, the ruler of the city, hunting with his court. He does not see the lovers at first; instead he and his friends expend twenty-one lines of dialogue on the subject of his hunting dogs, which—as it turns out—have been bred so that the several notes of their voices make a musical chord when sounded together. The lovers awake. Egeus, the father of one of them and a member of Theseus's entourage, repeats his accusation that one of the young men has stolen his daughter from her intended husband (who is at the moment in the arms of the other young woman in the group of lovers). Theseus, graciously accepting facts as they are, overrules Egeus and decrees that the two couples will be married along with him and his bride-to-be, Hippolyta.

How are we to react to this episode? If we think of it in terms of the kind of synopsis provided above, it becomes very simple. The captain of the citadel of reason journeys to the wood (the word 'wood' also means 'mad' in Medieval and Elizabethan English) and restores order to the chaos he finds there. His reference to his tuned dogs reinforces our impression that he, at least, can impose human patterns on natural forces. We may even recall, as Shakespeare almost certainly wants us to, a similar scene in Chaucer's 'The Knight's Tale'. Palamon and Arcite have met in a wood outside Athens to fight each other for the love of Emelye. Their combat is totally without rules, and Chaucer describes them as wild animals:

> Thou myghtest wene that this Palamon
> In his fightyng were a wood leon,
> And as a crueel tigre was Arcite;
> As wilde bores gonne they to smyte,
> That frothen whit as foom for ire wood.
> Up to the ancle foghte they in hir blood.[1] (1655–60)

Theseus discovers the two men in the course of his organised hunt for wild animals, and decrees that the fight for Emelye should be converted

[1] This and all subsequent passages from 'The Knight's Tale' are taken from F. N. Robinson, *The Complete Works of Chaucer*, 2nd. ed. (Oxford, 1957).

into a controlled contest, a tournament to which each man will bring 100 knights. The winner will marry Emelye. Again, the synopsis suggests a 'meaning'. The man of reason controls natural forces: unprincipled violence and eroticism are modified by the (relatively) civilised regulations for contests and weddings.

This is very much how readers and producers have seen Theseus's role in *A Midsummer Night's Dream*, and it is significant that in order to do so they too have had to reduce the play to the barest elements of its plot. The stage history of the play reflects this tendency. Of all Shakespeare's plays *A Midsummer Night's Dream* has been most frequently 'operatised', a process which subtracts subtleties of tone achieved through verbal juxtapositions just as inevitably as it adds music and machinery.

Purcell's *Fairy Queen*, for example, followed the plot of *A Midsummer Night's Dream* (except that it cut out Hippolyta and moved the mechanicals' play to Act III), but it used not one word of the Shakespeare text. In the performance of the opera in the Queen's Theatre in 1692, Act V culminated in a great audio-visual celebration of cosmic order. Juno appeared in a machine drawn by peacocks, alighted, and sang; a Chinese man and woman also sang. A grand dance included 'twenty-four Chineses', six monkeys and six pedestals supporting vases which contained six 'China-Orange Trees'.[1]

Garrick produced a version of the play, called *The Fairies*, at Drury Lane in 1755, keeping much of the text intact and introducing twenty-seven songs with lyrics borrowed from Dryden, Waller, Landsdowne, Milton and other Shakespeare plays. The entire mechanicals' subplot was excised, however, and so was Bottom. Another version, that was produced by Frederick Reynolds at Covent Garden in 1816, also added a good deal of song and subtracted whole episodes from the text: the scene with Helena in Act I was omitted; much of the lovers' dialogue was cut. Most important, the mechanicals' play was performed in the wood to allow space in Act V for a grand pageant of Theseus's triumphs, a procession of Cretans, Centaurs, the Minotaur, Ariadne 'in the Labyrinth' . . . even the ship Argo and the golden fleece.

The play suffered this kind of distortion even as late as 1856, when Charles Kean cut Act I, Sc. 1, from 251 to 161 lines, reduced Titania's speech beginning 'These are the forgeries of jealousy:' to 9½ lines and made heavy cuts in Act III. Puck's first speeches were given to a fairy so

[1] See George C. D. Odell, *Shakespeare from Betterton to Irving* (New York, 1920), Vol. 1, p. 194 and *passim*.

that Ellen Terry, as Puck, might be free to rise into view on a mushroom while music played.

These several versions of *A Midsummer Night's Dream* are very different from each other, but they share one common feature: they all attempt to smooth out complexities of tone in the original.

The Fairies, in cutting out Bottom and the other mechanicals, removed a means of parodying the lovers' behaviour and weakened the visual emphasis on Titania's infatuation. When Kean cut Titania's 'forgeries of jealousy' speech, he removed the most vivid reminder in the play of the fairies' horrifying power. Reynolds's version and *The Fairy Queen* both made room at the end of the play to express, through music and spectacle the idea of order achieved. By making the pageant a recapitulation of Theseus's triumphs Reynolds presented Theseus as the major instrument —possibly the exclusive instrument—of this renewed order; he even cut out the appearance of the fairies at the very end, by which Shakespeare gives the impression that they 'inherit' the world of the play and transcend the jurisdiction of Theseus.

When someone converts a play into an opera, he tends roughly to retain the play's structure—its plot, its sequence of events—and modify its 'verbal' elements. Irony is still possible, of course—two events placed side by side can comment on each other—but dramatic effects dependent on imagery, on different levels of language and their appropriate speech rhythms (what, for want of a better term, one might call the more 'literary' elements of the play) tend to get lost as the music, with its own rhythms and the 'imagery' of its melody, assumes greater importance.

In the 'operatic' versions of *A Midsummer Night's Dream*, then, the following events take place. The King of Athens announces his intention to marry the Queen of the Amazons, an action which will be seen as a way of re-establishing the proper feudal control of man over woman. But at the same time some adolescents are busy breaking other feudal relationships: they are disobeying their parents and their sovereign. The problem cannot be solved at home, so they escape into a fantasy world, an upside-down version of the world of Athens, where all kinds of unbelievable things happen to them. From this experience they emerge both more enlightened and more manageable, so that at the end of the play they can return to Athens ready to contribute to and participate in a more perfect order than existed when they left. Theseus is the chief exponent of this order, and its spokesman. This kind of summary has been the foundation not only of more than one opera but of useful generalisations about Shakespearean comedy (change a few details and names and you have *As You Like It*), and it is significant that Northrop Frye, for instance, makes use of terms drawn from opera and other musical forms in his interesting discussions of comedy as a literary form.[1]

As a way of examining how one play works, however, this sort of procedure has obvious limitations, and we can try to define them more clearly if we return briefly to the scene at which we started, the point where Theseus enters the wood to discover the sleeping lovers. In the first place, the lovers' problems have been, to an extent, sorted out before he enters. The fairies leave the lovers better off than they find them: the love juice in Demetrius's eyes is left uncancelled, so that at last he comes to love Helena. Just before Theseus enters, Oberon and Titania join each other in a dance, at the end of which Oberon says, 'Now thou and I are new in amity'. If we believe Titania's earlier remarks on the cosmic disorder engendered by their argument (and they are vivid enough to be immediately effective dramatically) we must take this affirmation of a renewed order as enormously important within the world of the play.

If this episode had occurred after Theseus's entry, the audience might feel that the fairies were making a hasty attempt to imitate the renewed order imposed by the return to the scene of temporal authority. Given the present arrangement, one gets a rather different impression. Theseus's first comment on what he finds before him is curious:

> No doubt they rose up early to observe
> The rite of May, and hearing our intent
> Came here in grace of our solemnity. (IV. I)

Our first reaction is that this account is wildly, even comically, far from the truth. The lovers have been engaged in nothing so controlled as a 'rite' (even a 'rite of May'), and far from concerning themselves with the respect due to their feudal lord, they have left Athens in implied dis-obedience to his wishes. Theseus, with his 'No doubt . . .' and his smooth enjambments, seems so coolly certain that he is right; yet we know he is wrong, and even his assumption that the feudal hierarchy must have been maintained (underlined by his use of the royal plural) shows that he inhabits a world very different from that of the wood.

Theseus's smooth certitudes become further undercut when Demetrius tries to explain what has really happened:

[1] See, for example, *A Natural Perspective* (New York, 1965), pp. 25ff.

> But, my good lord—I wot not by what power,
> But by some power it is—my love to Hermia,
> Melted as the snow, seems to me now
> As the remembrance of an idle gaud. . . .

Demetrius too wants to assert his role within the feudal system ('my good lord'), but something about which he is not at all certain keeps interrupting his train of thought. We feel that Theseus's experience, even though he too is a lover, is so remote from that of these young people that he cannot possibly understand what they have gone through. How, then, can he be so sure what has happened when they are not? Bottom's famous 'Man is but an ass if he go about to expound this dream' looks at first like an unconscious joke recoiling on Bottom himself, but the audience takes it also as an oblique comment on Theseus's certainty.

But our awareness of the disparity between Theseus and the lovers is only our first response. What we should recall, before too long, is that whatever his status now, Theseus himself has a past history of irrational love affairs conducted with as much violence and treachery as any lover has displayed in the wood. Oberon reminds the audience of these events when he accuses Titania herself of favouring Theseus:

> Didst not thou lead him through the glimmering night
> From Perigenia, whom he ravishèd,
> And make him with fair Aegles break his faith,
> With Ariadne, and Antiopa? (II. 1)

To what extent the attack on Titania herself is fair is never made clear (she dismisses Oberon's remarks as 'the forgeries of jealousy'), but Theseus's past exploits would have been known to the audience, and not only because they were recorded in Plutarch.

So our second response to the scene in which Theseus enters the wood is that perhaps he *ought* to know what the the lovers have been doing. Granted he has put all that behind him; now he has conquered those rebels against nature, the Amazons, and in a sense conquered the violence within himself as well. Moreover, he has allowed mercy to temper justice, at least within the governance of his private life:

> Hippolyta, I wooed thee with my sword,
> And won thy love doing thee injuries;
> But I will wed thee in another key. (I. 1)

But if this serene perfection makes him forget the facts of the other kind of love—the one which knows few rules and no reason—does it not ultimately limit his vision? Do not the lovers actually 'see' more, despite their blindness?

One tends to ask, rather than to answer, questions of this kind because of the extremely delicate balance of tone in the scene under discussion. For example, is it just our twentieth-century love of irony, combined with a slight knowledge of the background, that makes us suspect a hint of parody? Did Shakespeare hope the audience would bring to the play the traditional idea that Theseus represented orderly forces? Was he reminding the more cultivated among his audience of the similar scene in 'The Knight's Tale'? The reference to Theseus's tuned dogs especially prompts these questions. The dogs can be rationalised as an expression of the order Theseus represents, but is not this traditional association of Theseus with order (even the idea of order itself) pushed almost to the point of absurdity when it is made clear that the dogs are more decorative than useful?

> Crook-kneed; and dewlapped like Thessalian bulls;
> Slow in pursuit, but matched in mouth like bells,
> Each under each.

Remember also that this lengthy discussion interrupts a scene in which events have been moving rapidly (the fairies have removed Bottom's head, made up their quarrel, danced and departed), so that a twenty-one line discourse on dogs adds to the impression of the ineffectiveness of Theseus and his train.

So when Theseus appears to solve the lovers' problems at the end of Act IV, he is really only ratifying in human terms a solution already established by the supernatural powers. Shakespeare makes this clear not only in his arrangement of events (arranging the fairies 'new amity' *before* the entry of Theseus) but also by using various verbal devices to limit slightly the dramatic impression of Theseus's power. Of course, this is a very sketchy account of the end of Act IV and much more has to be said about the scene, but it should serve as a warning that *A Midsummer Night's Dream* is a complex play, that much of its complexity lies in the realm of authorial attitudes, and that these subtleties of tone are largely conveyed through verbal—as opposed to visual or structural—devices. Any reading or production which assumes that the author's attitude is conveyed solely through the sequence of events (which, in other words, ignores ways in which verbal effects cut against attitudes apparently suggested by the sequence of events) is a distortion of the play. This should be a caveat not only for 'operatisers' but for the much greater body of opinion which considers *A Midsummer Night's Dream* the ideal fourth-form text. These are the people who see the fairies as harmless, the lovers as slightly naughty children allowed temporary licence by Theseus, and the mechanicals as instruments of a rather detached buffoonery. Once again the trouble here lies in accepting the play's events at their face value—of assuming, for instance, that Theseus's return at the end of Act IV reasserts order in a chaotic world. Theseus himself may doubt the power of fairies, just as he underrates the validity of the lovers' experience at the beginning of Act V; producers may follow Theseus's lead and present the fairies in costumes as gauzy and insubstantial as possible. But we distort the play if we take Theseus's view of events as normative. A version recently put on in San Francisco dressed the lovers in codpieces which *lit up* whenever one of them expressed his undying love to another. It might have surprised the fourth forms, but it came closer to the truth of the play than the sort of production which causes words like 'delightful' and 'enchanting' to spring to the lips of the critics.

2. Character and Emblem

It may be that many, if not most, of the over-simple interpretations of *A Midsummer Night's Dream* stem from a failure to understand the way in which Shakespeare develops the characters in the play. Anyone expecting the kind of 'true-to-life' subtlety of personality with which Shakespeare endows characters in the other comedies will be disappointed at the thinness of detail in the 'personalities' of Hermia, Helena, Lysander, and Demetrius. Indeed the assumption is not uncommon that *A Midsummer Night's Dream* relates to the later comedies as a sort of apprentice piece, the play in which Shakespeare learned the techniques of developing 'fully rounded' characters which he was later to perfect in, say, *As You Like It*. This assumption may well explain the tendency to simplify the play (and the corresponding need to fantasticate it with spectacle and machinery), since anyone looking for richness of realistic detail and not finding it may be excused for underrating the complexity of what is left without it. The complexity of the play certainly does not consist in subtle distinctions of individual personalities, but before establishing the rather special nature of the play's difficulty, we must attempt to clear the air around this problem of 'character'.

The (obvious enough) fact is that when we talk of 'character' in *A Midsummer Night's Dream*, we mean something so radically different from 'character' in the other comedies that the play cannot usefully be considered as a stage in Shakespeare's development as a portrayer of fully rounded characters at all. In *As You Like It* (a useful contrast because the plot is very roughly similar to that of *A Midsummer Night's Dream*) Rosalind and Orlando, Jaques, Celia, even Duke Senior are all recognisable as individuals, each with his own 'character'. With the exception of Silvius and Hymen, no character in *As You Like It* could be called a 'type'; no one 'stands for' anything. Indeed much of the interest of the play is focused on how these clearly individualised characters develop, and Orlando's education in the process of true love is thematically central. On the other hand, after reading or watching *A Midsummer Night's Dream* we have the greatest difficulty in remembering for long even important details about the characters. Which of the girls is forbidden by her father to marry which of the men? Who is the tall girl, and who is the short one? Who marries whom at the end? Their names seem little more than labels, as interchangeable as their alliances in the wood.

Indeed, with the exception of Bottom, 'character' in the play is not so much developed as defined:

> *Fairy:* Either I mistake your shape and making quite,
> Or else you are that shrewed and knavish sprite
> Called Robin Goodfellow. Are not you he
> That frights the maidens of the villagery,
> Skim milk, and sometimes labour in the quern,
> And bootless make the breathless housewife churn,
> And sometimes make the drink to bear no barm,
> Mislead night-wanderers, laughing at their harm?
> Those that 'Hobgoblin' call you, and 'Sweet Puck',
> You do their work, and they shall have good luck.
> Are you not he?
> *Puck:*
>   Thou speakest aright:
> I am that merry wanderer of the night. (II. 1)

This exchange sounds about as natural as the beginning of a music-hall routine (with 'Fairy' playing the straight man); it is crude, intrusive exposition written largely in end-stopped lines—reminiscent (or so it seems at first) of the 'early Shakespeare' of *Henry VI*. But there is an important difference: in *A Midsummer Night's Dream* certain passages in which the dialogue seems unrealistic are used deliberately, for specific effects. Elsewhere in the play the dialogue is 'natural' enough, in Act V, for example, or at the end of Act IV; but in passages which delineate character, as well as in some of the lovers' remarks in the wood, which we will examine later, Shakespeare chooses a more formal, even stilted style. In the case of Puck's introduction and first speech, the formal style suits the way his 'character' is presented: he is not allowed to develop into an individual with his own unique style. Instead he is described—in the first instance by someone else—according to certain traditional modes of behaviour. The passage reminds us (and might have reminded the play's original audience) of one of those Renaissance dictionaries that described mythological and legendary figures by a brief résumé of their lives and according to the moral values they presented.[1] The only difference is that here the subject is the 'mythology' of English folk-lore, not of antiquity.

The procedure of presenting character is even more strikingly 'unrealistic' in the case of the lovers. To define them Shakespeare describes the characteristic behaviour, not of them but of a traditional image for love, Cupid:

> Love looks not with the eyes, but with the mind,
> And therefore is winged Cupid painted blind.
> Nor hath love's mind of any judgement taste;
> Wings and no eyes figure unheedy haste.
> And therefore is love said to be a child
> Because in choice he is so oft beguiled. (I. I)

This is very like one of the little verses underneath the picture in an emblem book through which the iconology of the figure is defined. This exploration of the emblem for love ('Cupid' and 'love' are interchangeable by the logic of iconography as well as in the passage above) underlines our impression that everything the lovers are about to say or

[1] A late example, in English, is Alexander Ross, *Mystagogus Poeticus or the Muses Interpreter*, London, 1648. See De Witt Starnes and Ernest Talbert, *Classical Myth and Legend in Renaissance Dictionaries*, Chapel Hill, 1955.

do will be contained within the definition of the word 'lover'. We worry so little about individual personality that we feel no strain when Helena steps momentarily out of her role to deliver the choric statement above; we never think of asking, 'If she has such insight into the blindness of doting love, why does she act as she does in the wood?' because we have no sense of Helena's consistency as a person. Here she comments on the action, there she acts in it.

'The Knight's Tale', which can almost certainly be counted as a source for *A Midsummer Night's Dream*,[1] provides a notable precedent for this practice of defining rather than developing character. Palamon and Arcite, far from emerging as individual personalities, are defined in terms of the iconology of the 'oratories' at which they worship before their tournament. Palamon's patroness is Venus:

> For soothly al the mount of Citheroun,
> Ther Venus hath hir principal dwellynge,
> Was shewed on the wal in portreyynge,
> With al the gardyn and the lustynesse.
> Nat was foryeten the porter, Ydelnesse,
> Ne Narcisus the faire of yore agon,
> Ne yet the folye of kyng Salomon,
> Ne yet the grete strengthe of Ercules—
> Th'enchauntementz of Medea and Circes—
> Ne of Turnus, with the hardy fiers corage,
> The riche Cresus, kaytyf in servage.
> Thus may ye seen that wysdom ne richesse,
> Beautee ne sleighte, strengthe ne hardynesse,
> Ne may with Venus holde champartie,
> For as hir list the world than may she gye. (1936–50)

And Arcite prays to Mars; the narrator describes Mars's oratory:

> Al ful of chirkyng was that sory place.
> The sleere of hymself yet saugh I ther,—
> His herte-blood hath bathed al his heer;
> The nayl ydryven in the shode a-nyght;
> The colde deeth, with mouth gapyng upright.
> Amyddes of the temple sat Meschaunce,
> With disconfort and sory contenaunce.

[1] It is widely accepted as such by authorities on Shakespeare's sources, *e.g.* Kenneth Muir, *Shakespeare's Sources* (London, 1957), Vol. 1, pp. 31, 34. Shakespeare followed 'The Knight's Tale' closely when he collaborated with Fletcher to write *The Two Noble Kinsmen*.

Yet saugh I Woodnesse laughynge in his rage,
Armed Compleint, Outhees, and fiers Outrage. (2004-12)

This analogy between this and Helena's speech about Cupid is surely
quite close: the pictures are described, certain lessons drawn or implied
from them and the characters of the lovers fixed within the confines of
traditional emblems. Clearly Shakespeare was working within a tradition
(so, for that matter, was Spenser when he defined the attributes of Acrasia
in terms of the iconography worked into the ivory gates of the Bowre of
Bliss). The real question is, why did he choose to work within this
tradition? It was hardly that he or Chaucer were particularly inept at
developing individualised characters when they wanted to do so. Are
there any reasons—dramatic, thematic or otherwise—that prompted
Shakespeare to avoid realism in this play?

It might help to turn again briefly to 'The Knight's Tale'; why does
Chaucer choose not to present Palamon and Arcite as individuals? It
may be that he has quite deliberately designed the poem to give the
impression that from the point of view of their *moral* status, Palamon
and Arcite are virtually interchangeable.[1] Palamon and Arcite themselves
go to almost laughable lengths to draw distinctions between each other
—in the matter of their rival claims to Emelye, for example:

[*Palamon*]: I loved hire first, and tolde thee my wo
    As to my conseil and my brother sworn
    To forthre me, . . .
[*Arcite*]: For paramour I loved hire first er thow.
    What wiltow seyen? Thou woost nat yet now
    Wheither she be a womman or goddesse!
    Thyn is affeccioun of hoolynesse,
    And myn is love, as to a creature. (1146-8; 1155-9)

But the way in which Chaucer arranges the events in the story belies any
trivial differences between the two men. Everywhere episodes are
arranged symmetrically: both men fall in love with the same woman;
when Arcite is let out of prison and banished from Athens, he is convinced that Palamon is happier than he because he can see Emelye from
day to day, and he laments his fate; Palamon thinks Arcite the luckier
because he can raise an army in Thebes, make war on Athens and win

[1] Professor Charles Muscatine develops this idea convincingly in 'Form,
Texture and Meaning in Chaucer's *Knight's Tale*', *PMLA*, LXV (1950),
pp. 911-29.

Emelye, and he too complains of his fate. At the end of the first part the narrator asks what seems to be the customary *questione d'amore*:

> Yow loveres axe I now this questioun,
> Who hath the worse, Arcite or Palamoun? (1347–8)

But as the story develops—with Arcite and Palamon each fighting like animals in the wood, each making a long appeal to his divine patron, and each ranked against the other on opposite extremities of the tournament ring like contending vices in *The Castle of Perseverance*—the *questione* begins to look like a serious question about the lovers' relative moral status to which the answer must be, 'Neither'. And although the oratories and altars appear at first to distinguish the two men, both portray the same results of different causes: treachery, violence and sorrow.

If 'The Knight's Tale' were *Middlemarch*, the scene in which Palamon and Arcite argue over which of them really loves Emelye would be as direct a guide to the future development of their characters as the chapter in which Celia and Dorothea divide up their mother's jewels is to theirs. As it is, the only realistic or 'true-to-life' exchange between them becomes a false lead for the reader, suggesting distinctions between them as individuals which are later submerged by the identical moral implications of their behaviour. So Chaucer directs our attention away from character and towards the more abstract realm of moral values, thus in a very direct way forcing the reader to examine certain themes recurrent in the poem—concerns of different kinds of freedom and slavery. This ironic tension between, on the one hand, the men's apparent individuality and, on the other, their sameness in a realm other than that of 'character' is an important tactic for developing thematic concerns.

Shakespeare too draws our attention to surface differences between his lovers—distinctions which could be the basis for establishing them as individuals—only to undercut their seriousness. Quite late in the play, when the lovers' madness in the wood is fully developed, we suddenly learn that Hermia is shorter than Helena. (Presumably we have *seen* the difference in stature before, if the producer has chosen to emphasise it, but since the lovers have not mentioned it before now, we can take it that for them, at any rate, it has only just become an important issue.) At first the concern for size seems mainly symptomatic of Hermia's paranoia; she takes Helena's reference to her as 'counterfeit' and 'puppet' as attacks on her shortness, which they are not necessarily. But very soon the others pick up the cue until finally Lysander, long frustrated at being

unable to rationalise his sudden betrayal of Hermia, finds his pretext and
vents his really frightening aggression on her:

> Get you gone, you dwarf,
> You minimus of hindering knot-grass made,
> You bead, you acorn. (III. 2)

There are at least two ways—apprently opposite but, I believe, reconcilable—in which we can interpret this rather odd episode. It emphasises
the blindness of the lovers that such an obvious physical difference
between the women should have been overlooked by the men for so
long, and finally forgotten so suddenly and completely. Or, if we take
the different heights as only a surface distinction—with no bearing on
the relative moral stature of Hermia and Helena—the episode shows the
lovers clutching pathetically at apparent distinctions as a defence against
the haunting fear that perhaps each of them really is interchangeable
with another in other people's eyes. These readings are reconcilable
simply because the play chooses to emphasise both the physical and moral
blindness of doting love.

But the main point of interest here is that we should find this episode
odd or funny at all. We do so because it pulls against our experience of
the way in which 'character' has been developed thus far in the play; we
know we are not in a world where surface attributes—of physical stature
or of personality—make any difference. As in the case of Palamon's and
Arcite's argument about who 'loves' Emelye, we get a glimpse of realistic
character development only to be reminded of its irrelevance in the
context. If we try to compare Shakespeare's purpose with Chaucer's in
doing this, we run into difficulty because the tone—and ultimately the
subject matter—of *A Midsummer Night's Dream* is different from that of
'The Knight's Tale', but suffice it to say for the moment that Shakespeare
wants to show that whatever individuality people may cherish in themselves, certain basic impulses can make them behave very like other
people. Presenting his characters as devoid of indivudual personalities
is a useful way of translating this thematic statement into dramatic
terms. And in case we miss the point of how powerful forces can
occasionally turn characters into caricatures, Shakespeare actually lets us
see it happen in one case. Bottom, unlike the lovers, is allowed a personality, a style of language which establishes him as an individual like
characters in other Shakespeare plays. Yet he—most visibly and suddenly
of all—is turned into a type, a label, when his head is turned into that of

an ass; his speech remains distinctive, but he looses that part of his body which most directly conveys the nuances of human character, the face. What remains is an expressionless, inhuman mask. Here the polarities of realism and emblem are juxtaposed most sharply, as a guide to what is happening less obviously to the other characters, on whom powerful forces are working without their knowledge.

In *A Midsummer Night's Dream*, then, Shakespeare defines his characters according to what they represent, according to their labels. The lovers are not individuals, they are 'lovers', and the definition of that word will determine their behaviour; Puck's actions too are predicated by the definition of 'Puck'. Nor is the process restricted to characters; even places stand for something, are labels. Athens, established in literary tradition as the legendary seat of reason (in Boccaccio's *Teseida* and 'The Knight's Tale') is here almost a byword for rational order. The wilderness outside Athens is called a 'wood' and not a forest, as is the corresponding locale in *As You Like It*, because it must also be a label for 'mad', and in case we miss the point, Demetrius is made to pun on 'wood' (for 'mad' and 'forest') and 'wooed'; 'And here am I, and wood within this wood. . .'. With everything so clearly defined and with the infinite complexities of realistic character and 'real life' settings so firmly excised, no wonder those who came looking for realism go away convinced that the play is a little too simple.

What they have overlooked is perhaps the most important fact of the play: the ideas and forces which Shakespeare makes his characters (and even locales) represent are in every case morally ambivalent. To put it very simply for the moment, the powers which are personified in the figures of Theseus, Hippolyta, the lovers, the fairies, Athens, the wood, are presented as potentially both 'good' and 'evil'. This is the source of the rather unusual complexity of the play.

We might begin to illustrate this point by returning to the figure of blind love, Cupid:

> Love looks not with the eyes, but with the mind,
> And therefore is winged Cupid painted blind.
> Nor hath love's mind of any judgement taste. (I. I)

The 'mind' with which love 'looks' is not, of course, the rational faculty; this 'mind' is without balanced judgement, and would correspond more to emotional impulses, or the 'will' in Shakespeare's terminology. But the terms as well as the process of 'blind' love in Shakespeare, need some explanation. What follows is a very simplified version, but it will serve for the immediate purpose. The lover's senses, usually represented by the synechdoche 'eye', are affected by a lady's physical attributes:

> Tell me where is fancy bred,
> Or in the heart or in the head?
> How begot, how nourished?
> Reply, reply.
> It is engender'd in the eyes, . . .

as the song in *The Merchant of Venice* warns Bassanio while he surveys the caskets. 'Fancy' here is a delusory view of the whole person—traits of character as well as appearance—based on a brief assessment of appearance only. But the delusion is a product of what in medieval terminology was known as 'ymagynatyf', the mind's power to 'picture' what was not actually before the eyes, and another meaning for 'fancy' is, of course, imagination. The doting lover reacted so strongly to first impressions of appearance that he could go on to construct a synthetic person in his mind's eye after the real person had left his physical field of vision. Later, when he saw the 'real thing' again, he might not recognise it, so strong was the synthetic version built up in his imagination. This is the fullest sense in which 'fancy' is 'engender'd in the eyes', and it explains the apparent contradiction by which 'blind' love could also be called the 'love of the eye'. We are presented with two kinds of blindness, and they are not synchronous: in the early stage of doting love a lover committed the 'sin of the eye' by giving too much credence to visual stimuli, but this could also be called a kind of moral blindness, since the more important attributes of character were being ignored; in the later stage, the lover was cursed with an almost physical blindness, since his imaginative vision of the person (or his delusion) was so strong that he could no longer credit what he saw before him.

This is exactly what happens to Troilus, for instance. He falls in love with Cressida having seen her only, and not met her. While he waits for their first meeting, he worries that the imaginary picture of her in his mind's eye is already so powerful that the real woman will produce stimuli strong enough to overcome him:

> The imaginary relish is so sweet
> That it enchants my sense. What will it be
> When that the watery palate tastes indeed
> Love's thrice-repured nectar? (*T & C*, III. 2)

What actually happens is that the imaginary Cressida remains the only one for Troilus, and the character of the real Cressida goes unnoticed. He does his best to remake her in the image of what lives in his fancy:

> O! that it thought I could be in a woman—
> As if it can I will presume in you—
> To feed for aye her lamp and flames of love. (*T & C*, III. 2)

But the audience's awareness of the outcome—reinforced by the tentative syntax which Shakespeare gives Troilus in this speech—undercuts the hope heavily. When Cressida finally betrays Troilus and takes up with the Greek Diomedes, Troilus cannot believe his eyes, even when he sees the two of them together. It is worth quoting at some length from this scene, since it presents an unusually clear outline of what Shakespeare meant by doting love:

> *Diomedes:* What, shall I come? The hour?
> *Cressida:*   Ay, come:—O Jove!—
>   Do come:—I shall be plagu'd.
> *Diomedes:*   Farewell till then.
> *Cressida:* Good-night: I prithee, come.—
>   *Exit Diomedes*
>   Troilus, farewell! One eye yet looks on thee,
>   But with my heart the other eye doth see.
>   Ah! poor our sex; This fault in us I find,
>   The error of our eye directs our mind.
>   What error leads must err. O! then conclude
>   Minds sway'd by eyes are full of turpitude.
> *Thersites:* A proof of strength she could not publish more,
>   Unless she said, 'My mind is now turn'd whore.'
> *Ulysses:* All's done, my lord.
> *Troilus:*   It is.
> *Ulysses:*   Why stay we, then?
> *Troilus:* To make a recordation to my soul
>   Of every syllable that here was spoke.
>   But if I tell how these two did co-act,
>   Shall I not lie in publishing a truth?
>   Sith yet there is a credence in my heart,
>   An esperance so obstinately strong,
>   That doth invert the attest of eyes and ears,
>   As if those organs had deceptious functions,
>   Created only to calumniate.
>   (*T & C*, v. 2)

Shakespeare's treatment of blind love owes a good deal to medieval and renaissance moralisers on the theme of *Cupiditas*. The syntactical and verbal similarity between the following and what both Helena and Cressida say about doting love may indicate how closely Shakespeare was working within a tradition:

> Pingitur autem Amor puer, quia turpitudinis est stulta cupiditas, et quia imperfectus est in amantibus, sicut in pueris, sermo...Alatus, quia amantibus non levius aliquid nec mutabilius. Sagittas fert, quae at ipsae incertae sunt et veloces;... Ideo nudus, quia turpitudo a nudis peragitur; vel quia in ea turpitudine nihil est secretum.[1]

> (Now Love is painted as a boy because the desire for lust is foolish and because the speech of lovers is imperfect like the speech of boys . . . he is winged because nothing is lighter or more changeable than lovers. He carries arrows which themselves too are unsure and swift in flight . . . He is naked because lust is performed by naked people; or because in that turpitude nothing is secret.)

Before long Cupid's blindness became his most important attribute. He is blind, to paraphrase Berchorius's introduction to a commentary on Ovid's *Metamorphoses*, because he does not seem to mind on whom he he inflicts himself (since love can visit both poor and rich, ugly and beautiful, devout and lay) and also because men are blinded by him (since nothing is more blind than a man inflamed by love for a person or a thing).[2]

The main point to note here is that this form of love was always a 'bad' one and its blindness a distinctly pejorative attribute, stemming from a tradition of medieval iconography which associated blindness with evil, with spiritual and physical death.[3] A poet who wished to assert the enlightening nature of love had to argue against its blindness, to paint the picture of Cupid without the bandage over his eyes, as it were. There seems to have been no argument about possible 'good' and 'bad' meanings of blindness itself.

But in *A Midsummer Night's Dream* Shakespeare adopts this convention in which blind love is unambiguously 'bad' only to qualify it radically.

[1] 'Mythographus III', 11, 18, in G. H. Bode (ed.), *Scriptores rerum Mythicarum latini tres Romae nuper reperti* (Celle, 1834), p. 239. Quoted in Erwin Panofsky, *Studies in Iconology* (New York, 1939), p. 105n.

[2] T. Walleys, *Metamorphosis Ovidina moraliter . . . explanata* (Paris, 1515), Fol. VIII, v. Quoted in Panofsky, p. 106n.

[3] Panofsky, p. 110.

Helena's moral lesson on Cupid is set in a context that gives it a possible 'good' meaning too; just before her lines on Cupid's attributes, she says:

> Things base and vile, holding no quantity,
> Love can transpose to form and dignity.

The fact that love can change the ugly into the beautiful can be condemned or admired, according to one's point of view. Looked at in one way, it is obviously absurd, and Theseus makes it an occasion for satire at the beginning of Act V: 'The lover, all as frantic, /Sees Helen's beauty in a brow of Egypt.' But from another point of view it can be seen as an act of almost divine creativity, the means by which fallen nature can be redeemed, however incompletely and for however short a time. The lightning flash of love, as Lysander calls it (I. 1) is only 'momentany' and comes quickly 'to confusion', but while it lasts it illuminates 'both heaven and earth' as though in imitation of divine redemption. The act of transposing the ugliness of the world into the beauty of an imaginative construct is very similar to the art of poetry, as described by numerous contemporary essays defending the writing of fiction. Sidney makes a clear distinction between those whose 'Arte' is confined to the works of nature (like historians, astronomers and natural philosophers) and poets, who create their own nature in their imaginations:

> Onely the Poet, disdayning to be tied by any such subjection, lifted up with the vigor of his owne invention, dooth growe in effect another nature, in making things either better then Nature bringeth forth, or, quite a newe, formes such as never were in Nature, as the *Heroes, Demigods, Cyclops, Chimeras, Furies*, and such like.[1]

And the lover's 'fancy', which turns the fallen nature of his loved one into something better, is very like the poet's *furor*, which George Puttenham (and others) likened to the creative force of God Himself:

> A poet is as much to say as a maker. And our English name well conformes with the Greeke word. . . . Such as (by way of resemblance and reverently) we may say of God; who without any travell to his divine imagination made all the world of nought. . . . [2]

So Shakespeare's doting love can be ambivalent: a laughable delusion or an intimation of something truer than the literal world. In *Troilus and*

[1] *An Apology for Poetry*, London, 1595; in G. Gregory Smith (ed.), *Elizabethan Critical Essays* (Oxford, 1904), Vol. I, p. 156.
[2] *The Arte of English Poesie* (London, 1589), Smith *op. cit.*, Vol. II, p. 3.

Cressida it is important to the strategy of satire that the pejorative nature of blind love be stressed to the exclusion of its other aspect, but in *A Midsummer Night's Dream*, where the tone is more ambiguous, Shakespeare places the traditional moralisers' attack on Cupid in a context in which it is given double value. This ambivalence is thus imparted to the lovers.

Just as it helps to see the lovers of *A Midsummer Night's Dream* as types and the treatment of romantic love as a variant of a tradition, so it it useful to enquire what—if any—traditional ideas lie behind other characters in the play. The traditional ideas about Theseus, for example, were varied and complex. Medieval commentators saw the classical Theseus as a figure of either the rational or the irrational. As the betrayer of Ariadne and the hasty prosecutor of his son Hippolytus, he was an image of treachery and rashness. As the subduer of revolted nature in the shape of the Minotaur, the Centaurs, and the Amazons, and as the ruler of Minerva's city, he embodied reason and temperance.

Medieval commentaries developed the idea of Theseus as man of reason,[1] and the *Moralised Ovid* kept the Ariadne story current. Chaucer drew on these sources, and others, for two quite distinct portraits of Theseus—in 'The Knight's Tale' and in Ariadne's story in *The Legend of Good Women*. Lydgate's *Fall of Princes*, paraphrasing a French prose version of Boccaccio's *De Casibus Virorum Illustrium*, recounts Theseus's battles with the monsters and his trip to the underworld with Perithous to rescue Proserpina. Athens is described as sacred to Minerva 'for ther wisdom and ther sapience' and as the fountain, under Theseus's governance, of 'philosophie' and 'knyhthod'. But fortune turned against Theseus when he believed Phedra's accusation of Hippolytus and condemned his son to death. This was an error in judgement, a departure from the discretion and prudence necessary in the just prince.

The tradition was so varied that even the same events in Theseus's life could be moralised in opposite ways. After pointing out that Theseus's defeat of the monsters provides 'a fit example of valour and justice for Princes to imitate', Alexander Ross considers his descent to the underworld:

> [Theseus] going down to hell to ravish *Prosperpina*, where he was bound, and from whence he could not be delivered but by *Hercules*,

[1] For a brief account of this tradition in the medieval iconography of Theseus, see D. W. Robertson, Jr., *A Preface to Chaucer* (Princeton, 1962), pp. 260–4.

teaches us that lust and venery have brought many a man to sickness, and deaths door as we say.

And yet by this very act Theseus becomes no less than a type of Christ:

> Our blessed Saviour is the true *Theseus*, who was persecuted in his infancie, and in his life-time overcame many monsters, but far more in his death; hee went down to hell, and from thence delivered mankinde. . . .[1]

Shakespeare simplifies the issue by choosing, so to speak, the Theseus of 'The Knight's Tale' and excluding his alter ego in *The Legend of Good Women*. Shakespeare's Theseus is the man of reason and good government—both of self and of state. His rash acts, though it is important to the play's strategy that we should be reminded of them, are safely in the past. But just as he makes fancy and doting love ambivalent, so Shakespeare also gives a double meaning to the opposite value, reason, and to Theseus its representative. In Shakespeare's hands the very rationality of Theseus becomes ambivalent. However well it fits him for guiding the affairs of men in the world—of governing a city state—it restricts his view of romantic love, of poetry, or of anything which is at least partly the product of the imagination. In the terms of the play, the worlds of fancy and reason are opposed; hence the representative of reason misunderstands—or chooses to misunderstand—what he discovers in the course of his hunt in the wood, and he says in Act V that he does not believe the lovers' story.

It may be that Shakespeare took the idea of Theseus's ambivalent rationality from 'The Knight's Tale'. Chaucer seems to want to stress the limits of Theseus's 'reason'. The *sentence* of the famous 'Firste Moevere' speech ('Thanne is it wysdom, as it thynketh me,/To maken vertu of necessitee,') is a close translation of Boccaccio's 'E però far della necessitate virtù, quando bisogna, è sapienza, . . .' (*Teseida*, XII, 11). By 'vertu' Chaucer's Theseus, therefore, probably means fortitude or valour, a stoic value in an argument for stoic patience in the face of adverse fate. This is, however, a negative and rather chilly message, quite distinct from Christian patience, which derives from a transcendent view of God's redeeming providence. One mentions the alternative, Christian response to adversity, because Chaucer—as opposed to Boccaccio—seems to remind the reader of it. The story is being told to an audience of Christian pilgrims (to whose response the reader's attention is directed

[1] *Mystagogus Poeticus*, pp. 399–401.

from time to time), and the Knight draws an explicit comparison between their world and the pagan setting of his story when he describes Arcite's death:

> His spirit chaunged hous and wente ther,
> As I cam nevere, I kan nat tellen wher.
> Therfore I stynte, I nam no divinistre;
> Of soules fynde I nat in this registre. . . . (2809–12)

Chaucer's view of Theseus as the enlightened pagan without grace may have given Shakespeare the clue for an enlightened Theseus without imagination. In any case, the Theseus in *The Two Noble Kinsmen* is a prophet of fortune, not of providence, who closes the door firmly on speculations about things metaphysical:

> O you heavenly Charmers,
> What things you make of us? For what we lacke
> We laugh, for what we have, are sorry still,
> Are children in some kind. Let us be thankefull
> For that which is, and with you leave dispute
> That are above our question.

A similar ambivalence is generated in the way the fairies are presented, although the process is rather different. Whereas in the case of 'blind' love Shakespeare took a uniformly pejorative tradition and made it ambivalent, with the fairies he simply embraced all the meanings which a tradition held for his contemporary audience. It is very difficult to make accurate generalisations about what an Elizabethan audience thought about fairies, so sparse is the written evidence. An authority on the subject, K. M. Briggs, claims that an Elizabethan or Jacobean author could choose from four main types of fairies: the trooping fairies, the hobgoblins, mermaids and giants (or monsters and hags), and could regard them as forces of either good or evil.[1] Of the four types, the first two are by far the most important. The trooping fairies, the figures of Celtic myth and medieval romance, spent much of their time in heroic pursuits like hunting, hawking and riding in processions; they were usually, though not always, dangerous to human beings. Most of them were of human size or larger, though here again there were exceptions, such as Oberon, whose German name, Alberich, meant 'elf king' and who in the French romance, *Huon of Bordeaux*, was the size of a three-year-old child. The Hobgoblins, of which Puck is a representative, were

[1] *The Anatomy of Puck* (London, 1959), pp. 12–16.

usually smaller and less formidable than the trooping fairies, though still capable of mischief (Puck himself could be a devil as well as a sprite). Their jurisdiction was confined more to the household and farm; they helped with domestic chores, or punished housemaids and milkmaids who did not do their chores properly. Contemporary opinion considered that both types had descended from the pagan gods. James VI of Scotland wrote in his *Daemonologie* of 'That forth kinde of spirites, which by the Gentiles was called *Diana*, and her wandering court, and amongst us was called the *Phairie*',[1] and Arthur Golding's translation of Ovid's *Metamorphoses* renders 'fairies' for *naidas et dryadas*.

Dr. Briggs suggests that the hobgoblins had in Elizabethan times been very recently transmitted from oral to written tradition, possibly through the agency of the new yeoman writers, whose country folklore was mixed with the fairy tradition already established in romance, to stimulate a new vogue in the capital.[2] This is an interesting theory: certainly Shakespeare, whom Dr. Briggs would presumably include among the new class of authors, appears to be educating his audience in folklore in the passage in which Puck is introduced.

The problem for the modern critic, though, is not only that people seem to have attributed to the fairies widely differing moral values, but that the fairies were not, or course, taken uniformly seriously. We may assume that the less sophisticated among Shakespeare's audience retained at least a residual belief in the power of fairies, but what about the more educated? *The Faerie Queene* is hardly the product of a man who believed in fairies. It may be that the revival of interest in fairy-lore among the *literati* can best be understood in the light of a modern analogy, the fascination that vegetation myths had for certain writers in the era of post-Frazer anthropology; that is, they did not believe in them literally but saw them as a useful fiction for exploring certain human truths. Hence when Spenser writes in his *Epithalmion:*

> Let no deluding dreames, nor dreadfull sights,
> Make sudden sad affrights;
> Ne let house-fyres, nor lightenings helplesse harmes,
> Ne let the Pouke, nor other evill sprights,
> Ne let mischivous witches with theyr charmes,
> Ne let hob Goblins, names whose sense we see not,
> Fray us with things that be not:

---

[1] Edinburgh, 1597, p. 73.   [2] Briggs, p. 6.

he writes not for the superstitious but to recreate for the sophisticated a decorative version of old folk incantations, in which *genre* he finds convenient images for the sort of human impulses that could endanger a marriage.

For the ignorant, then, the fairies probably retained some of their power; for the more sophisticated, they became images for abstract forces, rather as the pagan gods do in 'The Knight's Tale'. Shakespeare's fairies elicit the widest possible range of responses from the audience watching *A Midsummer Night's Dream*. He makes them small, as though to suggest a certain beneficence, but retains much of their potential danger as well. Oberon and Puck, though capable of restoring order in the wood, also do their best to disrupt it. When Oberon says to Titania:

> Thou shalt not from this grove
> Till I torment thee for this injury, (II, I)

and:

> What thou seest when thou dost wake,
> Do it for thy true love take; . . .
> Wake when some vile thing is near! (II. 2)

we do not see him as merely impish or mischievous, but downright malevolent, hardly suiting the gauzy costume in which he is so often dressed. Again, although the fairies are small, their power seems limitless; the argument between Titania and Oberon produces sympathetic dissension in the cosmos, a most awesome 'progeny of evils' of which they are the 'parents and original':

> Therefore the winds, piping to us in vain,
> As in revenge have sucked up from the sea
> Contagious fogs which, falling in the land,
> Hath every pelting river made so proud
> That they have overborne their continents.
> The ox hath therefore stretched his yoke in vain,
> The ploughman lost his sweat, and the green corn
> Hath rotted ere his youth attained a beard. . . .
> The nine men's morris is filled up with mud,
> And the quaint mazes in the wanton green
> For lack of tread are undistinguishable. (II. I)

The speech is frightening because it suggests the fairies' wide-ranging influence not only over the elements, but—through control of the elements—over human beings too. The really disturbing thought is not that the fairies can create inclement weather, but that they can literally erase any trace of human order. They are, indeed, supernatural forces quite beyond the control of human beings. They, and not Theseus, finally establish order within the wood, and within the lives of the lovers; they, and not the mortals, close the play. Even at the end, when they come to bless the wedding, they remind the audience of their potential malevolence; the blessings they promise are negations of the evils that fairies traditionally brought to weddings:

> To the best bride bed will we,
> Which by us shall blessèd be;
> And the issue there create
> Ever shall be fortunate.
> So shall all the couples three
> Even true in loving be,
> And the blots of nature's hand
> Shall not in their issue stand.
> Never mole, harelip nor scar,
> Nor mark prodigious, such as are
> Despisèd in nativity,
> Shall upon their children be. (v. 1)

The ambivalence of the fairies can be more sharply illustrated by a slightly closer look at Titania. She is associated with the goddess Diana not only by James VI but by Ovid, who uses 'Titania' as an epithet for Diana in her guise as the sister of the Titan Helios, the sun god (*Metamorphoses* III, 173). Diana represented rather contradictory values: she was the moon goddess, the patroness of virginity and of the hunt but also—possibly through association with Lucina—the goddess of erotic love, of child-birth and of mutability. Shakespeare's 'Diana' embodies both the traditional equivalents: she is the chaste wife of Oberon, but she is also the goddess of child-birth of whose order the Indian woman was a votaress. Shakespeare emphasises her contrary roles by bringing them into conflict in the argument over the Indian boy. The ambivalence of Titania may also explain why the moon, Diana's emblem, stands for chastity when Oberon cancels the love juice—

> Dian's bud o'er Cupid's flower
> Hath such force and blessèd power (IV. 1)

—but stands for mutability and erotic love when Egeus accuses Lysander of having enchanted Hermia:

Thou hast by moonlight at her window sung
With feigning voice verses of feigning love,
And stolen the impression of her fantasy. (I. 1)

This, then, is what one means by the rather special complexity of
'character' in *A Midsummer Night's Dream*. The people in the play may
have been given labels rather than personalities, but their labels are
ambivalent in every case. The way in which Shakespeare uses the
traditions which he and his audience would share shows this ambivalence
to be deliberate: he either widens the implications of an idea, such as that
of blind love or Theseus's rationality, or accepts all its ramifications, as
with the fairies. The process may differ, but the result is the same. Even
Bottom's label, his ass's head, might have meant more than just merri-
ment to the audience; they may well have been reminded of Priapus,
by virtue of an old iconographic tradition that linked the emblem of the
ass with the erotic god.

This double value of character is crucial to the way we respond to a
play in which nothing is quite as simple as it seems at first. Much of the
play's ironic pressure consists in the audience's awareness, at any one
moment, of a character's contrariety: unless we remember the fairies'
potential evil even when they are acting graciously, unless we are aware
of the limits of Theseus's reason, unless we remember the potential
insights of blind love even when love seems most irrational and dangerous, we miss much of the point of the play.

3. Wood and Wit

The play begins with a conflict between generations. Theseus has no
sooner announced plans for his marriage than Egeus enters to accuse his
daughter of disobeying him. She prefers Lysander over Egeus's own
choice, Demetrius. Two kinds of relationship—between husband and
wife and between father and daughter—are thus mentioned within the
first twenty-five lines of the play. What do these two relationships have
in common? The answer will define the nature of the norms by which
Athens lives.

The Christian marriage, as the wedding service in the Book of

Common Prayer makes clear, is based on St. Paul's teaching that the relationship between husband and wife should imitate that of Christ and the Church: the husband should love his wife and she should obey him out of a reciprocal love. But other human associations—notably those of father and child, and master and servant, or in political terms, ruler and subject—should also reflect the union of Christ and Church. Paul even extends the analogy to the microcosm of the individual: our bodies should obey our heads (or our reason) just as the Body of the Church obeys its head, Christ.[1]

A Midsummer Night's Dream is hardly a Christian allegory, but it seems likely that Shakespeare depended on his audience's awareness of these Christian associations in order to establish with the greatest possible economy the norm from which most of the characters are soon to deviate. This would explain why the links between husband and wife, father and daughter, and reason and emotion are mentioned in such rapid succession in the first scene. Theseus comes on stage as a ready-made icon to support the Pauline authority of man over woman in marriage; he has defeated the rebellious females, the Amazons, and now prepares to apply this re-established order in his marriage to their former queen. But no sooner is this norm presented than we hear of another, similar relationship being violated: Hermia's filial bond of obedience to Egeus. Egeus accuses Lysander of having 'bewitched' his daughter with 'rhymes' and a 'feigning voice' and of having impressed his image upon her fancy; he is obviously preoccupied with the extent to which Lysander's various poetic tricks have made her imagination rebel against her reason. Theseus seems to support the distinction between fancy and reason and (naturally enough, as the head of Minerva's city) to prefer the latter:

> *Hermia:* I would my father looked but with my eyes.
> *Theseus:* Rather your eyes must with his judgement look.

Hermia can choose one of two men; one of them has the approval of her father, and one has not. Is she not unreasonable to choose the wrong one? Technically, yes, but in case the audience is tempted to disparage Hermia's criteria, Shakespeare gives the other side a voice almost immediately. Lysander answers that he is, by any objective test, as good a choice as Demetrius ('I am . . . as well derived as he, . . . My fortunes every way as fairly ranked . . .'), and that furthermore Hermia

[1] The relevant passage is *Ephesians* v, 6.

loves him; 'Why should not I then prosecute my right?' Why, indeed?
The question is unanswerable. Hermia and Lysander may be operating
according to the unpredictable dictates of the 'eye', choosing each other
without regard to practical advantage, but are the supposedly rational
criteria of Egeus any more explicable?

To put it another way, our main impression of Act I, when we see
it acted, is not that one or the other of the opposing sides is in the right,
but that things have gone generally wrong and the traditional values of
Athens—its civility, its orderly hierarchies—are no longer sufficient to
deal with the situation. Clearly what labour relations experts call the
'bargaining machinery' no longer works; nor do threats to implement
the law of the city (the options offered Hermia, either to marry Demetrius
or to face death or life in a nunnery, drive her further away from the
community, not back into it). In fact, if one had to summarise the action
of the first four acts of *A Midsummer Night's Dream*, one could describe
it as the process by which Athenian civility, now irrelevant to a new
situation, is gradually eroded and replaced with something else. Inexor-
ably the characters in the wood are forced to come to terms with forces
within themselves which they never knew existed and in the process
to disregard old social, verbal and fictional formulae which are no longer
adequate to deal with their new insights. In Act V they must apply their
new experience to living within the city once again, and this they do by
reassuming the city's standards. But Act V is a complicated matter, and
will be left to another chapter.

Perhaps we can best explore the process by which Athenian civility
becomes irrelevant in the face of new experience by looking first at the
subplot of the mechanicals' play. It is clearly bound up with the plot
of the lovers. The mechanicals' first rehearsal comes just after Hermia
and Lysander outline the paradoxes of 'true' love and decide to run away
together; their second rehearsal, which culminates in Bottom's 'translation', follows directly after the first transformation among the lovers,
in which Lysander is made to shift his attentions from Hermia to Helena.
The mechanicals' problems with their impending production get more
confusing as the perplexing events in the main plot occur more
frequently. The mechanicals' plot is, of course, a kind of parody of the
lovers', and this is to say that the two lines of action look at first very
different—even opposite—then gradually begin to display certain
similarities, so that one becomes a kind of comment on the other. At
first sight, for example, their 'lamentable comedy', with its violence and

its unhappy ending, seems very different from the courtiers' own action, yet it serves to remind the audience of dangers implicit in the lovers' behaviour. There is potential violence, even death, in the Athenians' love affairs too, and if we ignore this fact, we miss much of the ironic tension—and ultimately the meaning—of *A Midsummer Night's Dream*. Again, the mechanicals are putting on a play, and the Athenian lovers are engaged in 'real life', yet Puck calls the courtiers' antics a 'fond pageant', and they seem to assume new identities in the wood as freely as actors do on the stage:

> Hate me? Wherefore? O me, what news, my love?
> Am not I Hermia? Are not you Lysander? (III. 2)

The most persistent joke within the mechanicals' plot itself is that their cultural background, having denied them the experience of romantic love and the terminology to deal with it, suits them badly to performing *Pyramus and Thisbe*. Yet the Athenian lovers are as badly suited to their environment in the wood, and they too find their language unequal to describing what is happening to them.

The mechanicals demonstrate their unsuitability to the task of producing *Pyramus and Thisbe* in a number of ways. They misuse the high terms of melodrama; they have an excessively literal approach to the business of dramatic illusion. Their casting is haphazard: Flute is made to play Thisbe even though he has 'a beard coming' and—presumably—a voice changing; Bottom, gleefully disregarding any trace of casting propriety, offers himself for any role—human or animal, male or female, lover or tyrant. All this makes for a number of jokes within the scenes concerned (the best being, perhaps, that of the biter bit, when Bottom gets more than he bargains for in the way of masks to assume), yet it has a more serious side in the wider context of the play as a whole. The disorder and impropriety of the mechanicals fit well into a setting in which the Queen of the Fairies turns against her husband, two women forget their life-long friendship to compete aggressively for one man, and two men try to carve each other up in the darkness.

The mechanicals even provide a humorous echo of the lovers' linguistic tangles. In the last hundred lines or so of I. 1 the lovers express their bewilderment about love through a number of paradoxes. Here, for example, the two women discuss Demetrius:

> *Hermia:* I frown upon him, yet he loves me still.
> *Helena:* O that your frowns would teach my smiles such skill!

Hermia: I give him curses, yet he gives me love.
Helena: O that my prayers could such affection move!
Hermia: The more I hate, the more he follows me.
Helena: The more I love, the more he hateth me.

The paradoxes arranged antiphonally express the lovers' feeling that things are exactly the opposite of what they ought to be. Shakespeare echoes comically this sense of the inversion of the natural order when in the next scene he makes Bottom say exactly the opposite of what he means: 'generally' for 'severally', 'aggravate' for 'moderate', 'obscenely' for 'seemly'. The mechanicals too have their paradox and oxymoron: the play is called *The most lamentable comedy and most cruel death of Pyramus and Thisbe*; Bottom claims he can speak Thisbe's part in 'a monstrous little voice' and 'roar you as gently as any sucking dove' if he plays the lion. This is important because the audience comes to chart the progress or regress of the characters in *A Midsummer Night's Dream* in terms of how appropriate their language is to their experience. The linguistic jokes in the comic underplot, while being funny in themselves, serve to keep our attention fixed on the kind of language all the characters speak, and possibly even to provide an oblique comment on the language of the lovers specifically.

Even some apparently small details in the mechanicals' plot are important. The mechanicals are very preoccupied, for example, with the lion. Won't it frighten the ladies of the court? Shouldn't they devise some way of reminding the ladies that the lion is only make-believe?

> *Bottom:* Nay, you must name his name, and half his face must be seen through the lion's neck, and he himself must speak through, saying thus, or to the same defect: 'Ladies', or 'Fair ladies—I would wish you', or 'I would request you', or 'I would entreat you—not to fear, not to tremble. My life for yours: if you think I come hither as a lion, it were pity of my life.' (III. 1)

This all adds to the local joke of how unsuited they are to the craft they are trying to practise, but when set against the wider context of the larger plot, in which Bottom, transformed into an animal, will inspire love—not fear—on the part of the most delicate 'lady' of all, it becomes an ironic comment on the play's action. Bottom's elaborate courtesies, his exaggerated respect for the ladies' sensibilities, remind the audience of a world very different from that of the wood, and help us to measure the distance the characters have come from that world; unknown to

Bottom, the civilities for which he has such concern have been over-turned:

> *Demetrius:* I'll run from thee and hide me in the brakes,
>   And leave thee to the mercy of wild beasts.
> *Helena:* The wildest hath not such a heart as you.
>   Run when you will. The story shall be changed:
>   Apollo flies, and Daphne holds the chase;
>   The dove pursues the griffin; the mild hind
>   Makes speed to catch the tiger—bootless speed,
>   When cowardice pursues, and valour flies. (II. 1)

And Helena, far from being frightened of wild animals, thinks of herself as frightening them away:

> No, no—I am as ugly as a bear;
> For beasts that meet me run away for fear. (II. 2)

Of course she does not mean it literally, but Shakespeare seems to have a purpose in making her express her preoccupation in precisely these terms.

But let us return to the question of what happens in the main plot. I have suggested that the action in the wood consists of the characters gradually forgetting the civilities of Athens as they meet with new experiences, and that the change in the kind of language they speak both reflects and makes explicit the changes that take place in their awareness of what goes on around them. To summarise baldly for the moment, they enter the wood speaking in a highly organised, witty, complicated manner, and leave it speaking much more simply.

It is worth taking a closer look at their more formal, courtly level of speech—in fact , examining briefly the general subject of formal dialogue in Shakespeare's early plays.

One influential school of thought holds that Shakespeare developed as a dramatist by putting behind him the euphuistic dialogue of his earlier plays, in which 'formal considerations . . . prevail over the full development of emotion' and instead adapting a 'free speech rhythm to [a] fixed blank verse framework.'[1] This is fair enough as a general account, although it could lead the unwary student to overlook the many uses Shakespeare makes of the formal style. It is not only the vehicle for the aristocratic hierarchies and courtly spectacle of the early histories, or for

---

[1] D. A. Traversi, *An Approach to Shakespeare*, 2nd. ed. (London, 1957), pp. 18–19.

the high-flown sentiment of *Romeo and Juliet*; it is also a useful ironic device, a means of modulating subtly the audience's attitude to the characters speaking it. We can see this most clearly in cases in which the formal and colloquial styles are juxtaposed—purposely—in the same scene. The episode in *Richard II* in which the king is forced to give up his crown juxtaposes a man who speaks in this manner—

> Now mark me how I will undo myself:
> I give this heavy weight from off my head,
> And this unwieldy scepter from my hand,
> The pride of kingly sway from out my heart;
> With mine own tears I wash away my balm,
> With mine own hands I give away my crown,
> With mine own tongue deny my sacred state,
> With mine own breath release all duteous rites, (*R II*, IV. I)

with one who speaks at another level:

> On Wednesday next we solemnly set down
> Our coronation: Lords, prepare yourselves.

The comparison cuts both ways. Beside Richard's rhetoric, Bolingbroke's is clear, efficient, decisive; it is also crude—lacking the equipment for the fine moral discrimination which the situation demands of a complete human being. Against Bolingbroke's incisive commands, Richard's rhetoric seems empty, stagey, self-regarding, yet its balanced periods and parallel constructions, suggesting as they do a kind of anti-coronation ceremony, reinforce the idea that the anointed of God upon whose stability the whole state depends, is about to give his power over to a politician. When Bolingbroke asks Richard, 'Are you contented to resign the crown?' he answers with a pun on 'I' and 'ay':

> Ay, no; no, ay; for I must nothing be;
> Therefore no no, for I resign to thee.

But the wit, though we feel it is less appropriate in the context than good, straightforward speech, is not merely for pretty effect; Richard is trying to express as concisely as possible, a complex train of thought, of which the following is a simplified (and much less effective) paraphrase: 'If I answer yes to your question, it implies that I am content, which I am not; if I answer no (i.e. that I am not content), it will imply that I wish to hang on to the crown, which is—regrettably—impossible. You might as well have asked me if I had stopped beating my wife. Therefore my answer (to 'Are you contented . . .') is no, no (a thousand times) because you are forcing me to resign to you, and you might as well stop this pretence that I am handing over to you willingly. I also wish to imply "I? no; no 'ay'; for 'ay' must nothing be;" in other words, you will get no affirmative answer from me as a person because "yes" would convert me as an institution into nothing. Also "I? no; no 'I', for I must nothing be" and cannot take decisions of this magnitude if I am nothing.'

And so forth. Richard may be showing off, but his complex, witty poetry is the only instrument for expressing the conflicting moral protocols of the situation. His final, most searching insight is—characteristically—his most self-conscious: can even *he* uncrown himself? Is he, as a person, not the worst traitor of all when he undoes himself, as an institution? It is dramatic self-abasement, but it is accurate. Compared to Richard, the prosy Bolingbroke seems badly equipped to deal with the moral realities of the situation, however adequately he responds to its practical dictates. The high style defines for the audience Richard's weaknesses and strengths: his vain posing and his position as the upholder of a vastly civilised, sensitive, medieval order.

In *A Midsummer Night's Dream* too the courtly style is used both seriously and ironically—seriously, when the complexities of its tone, vocabulary and syntax are fully engaged to define the subtleties of love; ironically, when it is spoken by a character whose behaviour no longer squares with his view of himself. Early in the play, before the characters have left Athens, the high style seems well suited to the use made of it:

> *Lysander:* Ay me! For aught that I could ever read,
>   Could ever hear by tale or history,
>   The course of true love never did run smooth;
>   But either it was different in blood—
> *Hermia:* O cross!—too high to be enthralled to low.
> *Lysander:* Or else misgraffèd in respect of years—
> *Hermia:* O spite!—too old to be engaged to young.
> *Lysander:* Or else it stood upon the choice of friends—
> *Hermia:* O hell!—to choose love by another's eyes. (I. I)

This is a pretty display, a sort of courtly word game. The proposer offers a certain amount of information, divided into points expressed in parallel syntactic units ('but either . . . Or else . . . Or else'); the respondent takes up each of these points and fits them into an even more formal framework, extending the parallelism to include an apostrophe and an antithesis in each of her answers. The artificiality of this passage

suits it well to the several formal definitions of romantic love which Act
I provides for the audience; the balanced periods support the idea that
love imposes a kind of symmetry by pairing off individuals; the anti-
theses remind us that the match is often unequal. The formality also
expresses Lysander's and Hermia's attempt to buttress themselves against
the unknown trials of love awaiting them. By rehearsing an exaggerated
and inclusive account of the possible troubles of romantic love, one can
prepare for the worst. As for their present 'cross', it is comforting to
have it plotted against a general pattern, especially when the pattern
is drawn from stereotypes of hearsay and fiction which cannot possibly
apply to them personally.

Yet even at this early stage in the play the audience begins to be aware
of slight stresses within the formal style. In their little word game,
Hermia answers Lysander and appears to agree with him, yet her very
agreement interrupts his flow of ideas. There is an early hint here of the
tension between concord and discord which will electrify later scenes
in the wood. Again, she appears to control the raw materials of her
language, in that she makes her responses even more formal than his
propositions, yet her apostrophes become more violent as she proceeds
('O cross! . . . O spite! . . . O hell!'). The impression the audience gets
is that Hermia has a surging energy which is pulling increasingly against
the rules of the verbal game, just as it will strain and eventually break the
'rules' of Athenian civility.

The business of invoking stereotypes is pushed a stage further when
Hermia answers Lysander's plea to meet him in the wood

> My good Lysander,
> I swear to thee by Cupid's strongest bow,
> By his best arrow with the golden head,
> By the simplicity of Venus' doves,
> By that which knitteth souls and prospers loves,
> And by that fire which burned the Carthage queen
> When the false Trojan under sail was seen,
> By all the vows that ever men have broke—
> In number more than ever woman spoke,—
> In that same place thou hast appointed me
> Tomorrow truly will I meet with thee.

The burden of this speech is simply 'I'll be there'; the conventions of the
complex courtly style and the stereotype are, therefore, less useful to her
purpose than they were to Lysander's. Indeed, they even get in the way,

diverting the audience's attention from an otherwise direct line of statement and introducing associations, such as the violence of Dido's suicide, which Hermia cannot really intend. She does not seem entirely in control of her rhetoric.

When the lovers enter the wood the courtly style becomes still less suited to its surroundings and to the use to which it is put. We get the feeling that the more strictly the stereotypes of rhetoric and metaphor are observed in this new context, the less they actually communicate. Immediately before Lysander's transformation, he and Hermia, having lost their way, look for a place to spend the night. He wants to join her on a bank;

> One turf shall serve as pillow for us both;
> One heart, one bed, two bosoms, and one troth. (II. 2)

Hermia is uneasy about the idea and for modesty's sake would rather lie further off. He answers:

> O, take the sense, sweet, of my innocence!
> Love takes the meaning in love's conference—
> I mean that my heart unto yours is knit,
> So that but one heart we can make of it.
> Two bosoms interchainèd with an oath—
> So then two bosoms and a single troth.
> Then by your side no bed-room me deny,
> For lying so, Hermia, I do not lie.

As Hermia says, 'Lysander riddles very prettily'. Something about his speech suggests the conventions of love poetry—its puns, its figures to suggest the union of two in one, its promise of troth, its tactic by which the persuasion to physical love is wittily disguised as part of a discourse on metaphysical concepts. But the main feature of witty love poetry is that although it appears 'difficult'—presents a complicated line of argument or a far-fetched comparison—it then resolves itself, so that one can say there is a sense after all in which these two things can be compared, or in which this argument does lead to that conclusion. Lysander's speech does not resolve its tensions, possibly because he rather fussily insists on the convention which admits the union of two hearts but refuses to allow 'bosoms' to combine as well. In the context of a discussion on where they will really lie for the night, the mixture of literal and figurative strikes an odd note. 'I do not lie' in the last line means 'I am not untrue', but to what?—to her concept of propriety which entails that they sleep apart, or to her? If the former, how does the preceding argument lead to this conclusion (or have any bearing on it whatsoever)? If the latter, how can it reassure Hermia, since being true to her and assaulting her—even rudely and physically—are not inconsistent procedures? The answer is, of course, that Hermia is not reassured and adheres to her original decision to sleep apart. She is probably as uncertain as the audience as to what Lysander means.

The language in this passage is further undercut by the context in which it is placed. Even the use of the courtly style itself is faintly absurd in a setting so remote—in distance and moral status—from the court. Then there is the fact that the episode is introduced by Lysander admitting he has lost his way. The more learned among the contemporary audience might have heard an echo here of the first book of *The Faerie Queene* (or *The Divine Comedy*, for that matter), in which losing one's way in a dark wood means wandering from the path of truth, and they might have appreciated the irony when (three times in the passage) Lysander talks so confidently of 'truth' or 'troth'. The two words could be used interchangeably in Elizabethan English,[1] and could mean either faithfulness or the facts as they are, so that keeping troth was both an intellectual and a moral act. The second line that Lysander speaks after his entrance, therefore, contains a sort of comic contradiction: 'And—to speak truth—I have forgot our way', and the fact that they have lost way (in the intellectual and moral sense provided by the allusion to the wood of Error) continues to negate all the smooth assertions and promises that follow.

In case we miss the point, the comedy is broadened almost immediately. Puck puts the love juice on Lysander's eyes, and Helena comes into his sight just as he wakes. The transformation is sudden and complete:

> Content with Hermia? No, I do repent
> The tedious minutes I with her have spent.
> Not Hermia but Helena I love.
> Who will not change a raven for a dove?
> The will of man is by his reason swayed,
> And reason says you are the worthier maid.
> Things growing are not ripe until their season;
> So I, being young, till now ripe not to reason.

[1] The First Quarto uses 'troth' throughout this episode. The New Penguin Shakespeare text uses 'truth' in line 42 and 'troth' in lines 48 and 56.

And touching now the point of human skill,
Reason becomes the marshall to my will. . . .

The obvious joke—that he thinks he is acting rationally when he is really following impulses started by the love juice—is enriched for us by a view of the formal style at its most pompous. Now the carefully balanced sense units have degenerated into heavy end-stopped lines, and the couplets, instead of exploring further the subtlety of the subject, undermine it by juxtaposing unlikely combinations: 'reason', which we (and Lysander) think of as the faculty for discerning permanent value, goes badly with the suggestion of flux which 'season' carries, and one does not normally think of the will embodying 'skill'. There is more 'love poetry' too, more stereotyped than ever. Lysander invokes that well-worn rhyme of 'love' and 'dove' with which Mercutio baits Romeo, and the claim to be acting according to the dictates of reason is almost as much of a convention in love poetry as the plea to throw reason to the winds.

The scene ends on a more serious note, however. Hermia wakes, on a stage now deserted, from a frightening dream in which a snake eats at her heart. The Lysander for whose help she calls is no longer the same person, and he is no longer there. His parting remark to the sleeping Hermia ('Of all be hated, but the most of me') was funny when he said it. Now, when Hermia shares with us her private vision of a rapacious, irrational animal preying on human beings, the dangerous implications of Lysander's comic misdirection becomes more apparent. It is funny that he should act as an animal and talk as a human being—that he should break their 'single troth' at the first sight of another woman; it is also frightening, when we are allowed to share the victim's viewpoint. A rigidly Christian critic might be tempted to connect Hermia's serpent vision with the Fall. Whether or not one wants to go this far, it is difficult to ignore one important similarity: whatever happens in the future, the relationship between Hermia and Lysander can never be quite the same again. Lysander has lost what he called 'my innocence', and Hermia's feeling of loss at his absence is perhaps the first great shock of her life. It is also the first step towards a new understanding of love.

To dramatise the process by which the courtly style degenerates as the lovers proceed through the wood, Shakespeare provides Helena as a point of contrast. Even at the beginning of the play she experiences a kind of 'cross' in love which the audience takes as more serious than that of Lysander and Hermia (they lack parental approval but she lacks a lover). Her behaviour—at least until the point at which all four of the young lovers finally abandon all traces of courtesy—exhibits a certain civilised scepticism when she rejects the impulsive advances of Lysander and Demetrius. This qualifies her to act—temporarily, at least—as authorial voice, as when she defines the nature of romantic love by an elaborate evocation of the emblem of Cupid in which the rhymed couplets exactly reflect the ironies she wants to convey. When she stops acting as chorus and re-enters the action, her use of conventional formulae provides the audience with as much information about her as about the subject she is discussing. Yet her 'message' is still efficiently conveyed:

> Run when you will. The story shall be changed:
> Apollo flies, and Daphne holds the chase;
> The dove pursues the griffin. . . . (II. 1)

She has had enough personal experience of the 'crosses' of love to know that the stereotypes can occasionally be inverted, but not enough to banish them from her consciousness altogether. This may represent an intermediate stage in her development, a point half-way between accepting the norms of fiction as the literal truth of her own experience and using the facts of the individual consciousness as the starting point for a fresh view of reality.

In any case, Helena's integrity is maintained until well after the other characters have 'gone mad' in various ways. Even when the four of them meet (after Lysander has abandoned Hermia, and Demetrius too has received the juice of Cupid's flower), she still speaks with the voice of sanity, trying to remind the others—through the medium of the courtly rhetoric which they have come to abuse—of the gentler age which they all once shared:

> We, Hermia, like two artificial gods
> Have with our needles created both one flower,
> Both on one sampler, sitting on one cushion,
> Both warbling of one song, both in one key,
> As if our hands, our sides, voices, and minds
> Had been incorporate. So we grew together
> Like to a double cherry, seeming parted
> But yet an union in partition,
> Two lovely berries moulded on one stem,
> So with two seeming bodies but one heart,
> Two of the first, like coats in heraldry,

> Due but to one, and crownèd with one crest.
> And will you rent our ancient love asunder,
> To join with men in scorning your poor friend? (III. 2)

It is very important to distinguish between this and Lysander's 'One heart, one bed, two bosoms, and one troth'. Helena's wit does resolve itself; the image of the double cherry makes quite precise the meaning of 'two beseeming bodies but one heart'. They are two people, but common nurture (the stem of the cherry, if one likes) made them as close as two individuals can be. The heraldry image reinforces this notion and places their 'ancient love' within the context of the medieval, hierarchical world of Athens. The speech is a moving cry of puzzlement and grief.

But it has no effect on the others. They continue, for a few more lines, to use the formal style to accompany the most informal actions. The men prepare to fight a duel over Helena:

> *Lysander:* Helen, I love thee. By my life I do.
>   I swear by that which I will lose for thee
>   To prove him false that says I love thee not.
> *Demetrius:* I say I love thee more than he can do.
> *Lysander:* If thou say so, withdraw, and prove it too.

Lysander's 'To prove him false . . .' is a general formulation, but it can apply only to Demetrius. His '. . . prove it too' rhymes with Demetrius's 'do', suggesting concord when he intends discord. The gap between manner and matter is at its widest at this point in the play. The tension is so great that the courtly style finally snaps. Now the microcosmic society of the four lovers adheres no longer through the subtle agreement of rhyme and metre, but turns directly upon itself. Lysander dismisses Hermia, not with the well-mannered hints he has tried before, but in a savage burst of verbal machine-gun fire:

> Away, you Ethiope! . . .
> Hang off, thou cat, thou burr! Vile thing, let loose,
> Or I will shake thee from me like a serpent.

We recall her dream. She, at last, gets the point, and her answer might stand as epigraph for the whole scene:

> Why are you grown so rude? What change is this,
> Sweet love?

The pace quickens as their actions and language become more basic, more 'rude'. Names, like other words, lose their conventional significance:

Hate me? Wherefore? O me, what news, my love?
Am not I Hermia? Are not you Lysander?

Suddenly their physical appearance becomes enormously important;
Lysander notices Hermia's dark complexion, and Hermia imagines
Helena insults her for her small stature. Later both Helena and Lysander
warm to her theme and really do taunt her with her size. Saddest of all,
perhaps, Helena herself becomes infected with the general malevolence:

O, when she is angry she is keen and shrewd.
She was a vixen when she went to school. . . .

So their common childhood was not an unmixed joy, after all; or is she
just telling a lie to serve the moment? Here the contrast between courtly
and barbaric behaviour becomes most pointed: even the patient, peace-
making Helena, who only a short time ago invoked the harmonies of
their past friendship in the balanced, complex rhetoric of the court, is
willing to abandon both loyalty and manners when she finds them
disintegrating in others around her.

Oberon and Puck intervene at this point. The misunderstanding is
discovered and will be put right: Lysander's infatuation for Helena will
be cancelled, and Demetrius' will not. The men will be made to chase
each other around the dark wood, but under controlled conditions and
only so that they will exhaust themselves and fall asleep. 'The man shall
have his mare again,' as Puck says, 'and all shall be well.'

But not before we get one final look at the world of unreason. The
subplot continues to amplify the oscillations of the main plot. The scene
immediately following, in which Titania makes love to the transformed
Bottom, is both more sharply comic—because of its visual arrangement
—and more terrifying than the lover's quarrel in the wood. Furthermore,
Titania's imagery is more sexually suggestive than any allowed the
the courtiers:

Sleep thou, and I will wind thee in my arms.
Fairies be gone, and be all ways away.   *Exeunt Fairies*
So doth the woodbine the sweet honeysuckle
Gently entwist; the female ivy so
Enrings the barky fingers of the elm.
O, how I love thee! How I dote on thee! (IV. I)

Even Oberon is moved to pity. But the word 'dote' reminds the audience
that this scene is only a more exaggerated presentation of the danger and
absurdity implicit in the courtiers' behaviour. Our relief at the solution

to their problems is the greater when we are allowed this oblique, retrospective image of their misdirection.

The entrance of Theseus and his court, with its talk of 'musical confusion/Of hounds and echo in conjunction' seems to reassert the values of Athenian civility over the chaos of the wood. Discords are made concords. Yet, as has been suggested before, the fact that Oberon has settled the lovers' problems already implies that the wood itself is capable of evolving its own order and that Theseus's role can be at best to ratify Oberon's order in the terms Athens understands. For the moment our interest must be concentrated on what the lovers say when they awake. Their first words fall naturally into the framework of the balanced court rhetoric which they know Theseus expects, but very shortly the pattern is modified:

> *Lysander:* My lord, I shall reply amazedly,
> Half sleep, half waking. But as yet, I swear,
> I cannot truly say how I came here.
> But as I think—for truly would I speak—
> And now I do bethink me, so it is:
> I came with Hermia hither. . . .
> *Demetrius:* But, my good lord—I wot not by what power,
> But by some power it is—my love to Hermia,
> Melted as the snow, seems to me now
> As the remembrance of an idle gaud. . . . (IV. 1)

The new feature of their language is a congruence of rhythm and meaning, so that (in this case) the burden of their speeches—their uncertainty—is reflected, as it would be in real speech, by rhythmic stops and starts, caesurae and enjambments. The lovers have discovered not only themselves and their rightful partners, but a new rhetoric in which manner and matter at last become fused.

What have they learned? It is easier to say what they have unlearned. They have left behind them their theories of love, their certainty that they know exactly what they are doing. Their theme now is 'truly would I speak' (the conditional mode is as important as the words) and 'I wot not'. Their language, once a stylised pattern of words which took little account of what was being conveyed by those words, has been broken down into its consituents and rebuilt:

> *Hermia:* Methinks I see these things with parted eye,
> When everything seems double.
> *Helena:*   So methinks,

And I have found Demetrius, like a jewel,
Mine own and not mine own.

Set against the paradoxes of an earlier era in their lives, this has the ring
of personal experience. At last they have found their own way of
describing the contradictions of romantic love, and at last they fully
apprehend its ambivalence. Their greatest wisdom at this stage is to
avoid hasty generalisations about their experience, to eschew casting
their impressions too quickly in a verbal mould. Whatever questions
their adventures may prompt—from Theseus or his court, or even from
each other—their safest answer, for the moment, is Bottom's to the
mechanicals: 'Not a word of me!'

4.   Strategic Puzzles

A tragic hero occupies uneasily a territory between utter depravity
and complete perfection. He must not be base, or his fall would simply
please us; he must not be totally good, or we would reject his downfall
as too much like the fallen world we all inhabit (we often witness
good people coming to grief in real life, but would not accept it in
tragedy). The hero is given this ambivalent status in order to direct the
audience's attention to a kind of action appropriate to tragedy—the
operations of fortune or divine justice. The extent to which we feel he
'deserves' his fall is the extent to which we are made aware of a divine
justice punishing his transgression; in so far as he does not deserve it,
we sense the presence of blind fortune which—in classical tragedy, at
least—not even the god scontrol.

The Shakespearean character, too, partly deserves and partly does not
deserve what happens to him. Comedy ends in a situation of renewed
order and social stability; for the audience to be convinced that this is
permanent, they must have been shown the characters working towards
the solution, undergoing a kind of initiation into the rites of the new
society. But the audience must also be reminded of the process of divine
mercy, which Shakespeare's comic action imitates to the extent that his
tragedy does divine justice. Thus the ending of a comedy seems more
perfect than anything the characters could have achieved working on
their own, or could ever understand completely.

So just as a tragic hero both deserves and does not deserve his fall, a comic character both deserves and does not deserve his rescue from the fallen world. This balance can be demonstrated clearly in a comedy like *As You Like It*, in which characters develop markedly. The deprivations of the forest teach Orlando important truths about civility and love, so that the audience feels he has earned the right to marry Rosalind. Yet neither he nor even Rosalind—despite her power to transcend her normal appearance to tutor Orlando and stage-manage the charade which brings the lovers together at the end—can be the sole agent of the comic solution. None of the human characters—however much he has learned —could possess the moral and intellectual power to engineer such perfection. Shakespeare emphasises the function of providence, in the case of of *As You Like It* by actually bringing in the supernatural, in the form of Hymen, as plausible author of the renewed order;

> Peace, ho! I bar confusion:
> 'Tis I must make conclusion
> Of these most strange events. (*AYLI*, v. 4)

In *A Midsummer Night's Dream* we are less certain how the characters develop, or indeed if they can be called 'characters' at all in the accepted sense of the word. Yet something enormous and frightening happens to them, and they respond by developing a style more fitting their new situation. This achievement is sufficient to make them plausible inheritors of the renewed order in Athens. But one is reminded of providence here too, not only directly through the visible intervention of the fairies, but indirectly through seeing the humans not entirely deserving or understanding the happy ending which they help bring about.

The lovers deserve this new world because they have suffered and because they are now convinced of the need to maintain the Pauline hierarchies of Athens. They will obey Theseus, marry, and submit their affections to the control of reason. To demonstrate how completely they have reassumed the values of the city, the Athenians put the world of unreason behind them. Theseus has already forgotten his adventures with Antiopa and Ariadne and averts his eyes from evidence of similar antics on the part of the younger lovers, when he finds them sleeping in the wood and when he dismisses their story at the beginning of Act V. The four lovers, presented with a pageant that should remind them of their misadventures in the wood, satirise it instead. It is quite right that they should do so. If they are to be seen to accept the canons of order, they must reject not only the dramatically inappropriate mechanicals' play, but the disorder which that play would represent if it *were* dramatically effective.

But in putting behind them all things unreasonable, the Athenians banish not only delusion but also whatever partial glimpse their imagination may have afforded them of Sidney's 'golden world'. This limitation in vision may be conscious and necessary, but the audience still feels it as a limitation; in being reminded of what the courtiers have forgotten, we come to realise what we have learned. The humans' assumption that they have worked out their own solution emphasises—by contrast— the beneficent power of the superhuman. The process by which Shakespeare limits the human characters in order to suggest the providential power of the supernatural is the 'action' of Act V, and it requires detailed examination.

Theseus and the lovers are limited when they—in their different ways —reflect on what happened in the wood. Theseus takes the most sceptical view of the story the lovers tell:

> I never may believe
> These antique fables, nor these fairy toys.
> Lovers and madmen have such seething brains,
> Such shaping fantasies, that apprehend
> More than cool reason ever comprehends.
> The lunatic, the lover, and the poet
> Are of imagination all compact.
> One sees more devils than vast hell can hold.
> That is the madman. The lover, all as frantic,
> Sees Helen's beauty in a brow of Egypt.
> The poet's eye, in a fine frenzy rolling,
> Doth glance from heaven to earth, from earth to heaven.
> And as imagination bodies forth
> The forms of things unknown, the poet's pen
> Turns them to shapes, and gives to airy nothing
> A local habitation and a name. (v. 1)

The rhetoric of this speech clearly places lovers, madmen and poets in the same category. Theseus means to satirise all three equally for their over-active imaginations. But to the attentive audience Theseus says more than he intends to. Shakespeare makes him echo unwittingly two remarks spoken earlier in the play: Lysander's description of love as a lightning bolt which 'unfolds both heaven and earth' and Helena's observation that 'Things base and vile, holding no quantity,/Love can

transpose to form and dignity.' The tactics are superb. We are invited
to balance Theseus's dismissal of imagination as merely delusive against
the opposite view of imagination as a vision of a better world. Theseus
wants Hippolyta, to whom he is talking here, to take 'fine frenzy'
ironically; the audience is free to take it seriously. He wants to place
poets and madmen in the same category; we can, if we like, find a real
distinction between looking towards hell and towards heaven, especially when the latter vision is made concrete in the 'local' image. For him
seeing a gipsy as Helen of Troy is absurd; for us, granted the gipsy's
point of view, it is as close as human beings can come to redeeming the
ugly world.

Theseus twice distinguishes between apprehension and comprehension
—once in the lines quoted above and again later in this same speech.
Comprehension is the art of generalising, or relating things to categories;
it is one of the tools of reason. The *O.E.D.* illustrates the verb by citing
Chaucer's translation of Boethius:

> '[Resoun] comprehendeth by an universal lokynge the commune
> spece that is in the singuler peces. . . .'

Apprehension circumvents the process of reason; it is the sudden,
inexplicable knowledge that a thing is so. According to Aquinas, it is the
way angels think, and Hamlet grants the faculty to men, at their best:

> What a piece of work is a man! . . . how express and admirable! in
> action how like an angel! in apprehension how like a god! (*H*, II. 2)[1]

Theseus's distrust of apprehending accords well with his role as ruler of
Athens, and it provides an important clue to his view of the world. He is
adept at generalising, at 'comprehending'; he looks constantly beyond
the specific fact to the category or 'kind' to which it belongs. In Act I,
when he tries to convince Hermia that 'Demetrius is a worthy gentle-
man' and she answers (convincingly), 'So is Lysander', he says:

> In himself he is;
> But in this kind, wanting your father's voice.

The word 'kind' appears again in Act V, in the course of a discussion
between Theseus and Hippolyta about whether the mechanicals should

---

[1] This is the Folio version. The punctuation of the Second Quarto links
apprehension with angels, not gods:

. . . how express and admirable in action, how like an angel in apprehension, how like a god.

be allowed to produce a play which is clearly going to be beyond their capacities:

> *Hippolyta:* He says they can do nothing in this kind.
> *Theseus:* The kinder we, to give them thanks for nothing.

But Theseus makes a serious point too:

> For never anything can be amiss
> When simpleness and duty tender it.

As a good generaliser he can see beyond the imperfect thing to the perfect devotion which it represents. Later, when Hippolyta finds the mechanicals' play 'the silliest stuff that ever I heard', Theseus generalises once again:

> The best in this kind are but shadows; and the worst are no worse,
> if imagination amend them.

Theseus is a politician, in the widest sense of the word—a master in the art of living in and governing a society. From a diplomatic point of view, each of these three generalisations—and much more he says besides —exactly suits the occasion which calls for it. Once Egeus has invoked the law against his daughter, Theseus must be seen to uphold it, but he must, if possible, placate the younger generation too by explaining the law in the gentlest possible terms. He assesses the mechanicals' play not on the grounds of its quality as a performance but for its political implications—what it tells him about their attitude to their ruler. His response to Hippolyta ('The best in this kind . . .') is a diplomatic refusal to enter into controversy at a moment when the players are doubtless watching him anxiously to see how he likes their play. The ruler of the rational society is also a little weary of the performance, 'yet in courtesy, in all reason, we must stay the time'.

But we would miss the point if we saw anything more in these statements than a sensitive, practical response to an immediate situation. Take the case of his advice to Hermia. From the standpoint of one who wants to uphold the Athenian hierarchy and mediate between father and daughter, it makes sense to look beyond the 'fact' of Lysander himself to his lack of parental support. But for Hermia, who sees only the man Lysander, the 'kind' to which he belongs—especially such a negative one as this—can only be irrelevant. Theseus responds to the situation as best he can, but the really complete response would have to take account of the particular as well as the general. Again, 'The best in this kind are but shadows . . .' is not a profound statement about art, though it has been taken as such by some critics. In so far as it is true, it is a truism, since it is obvious that all art is a copy. In so far as it is not a truism, it is misleadingly restrictive. Theseus denigrates the artistic copy with the limiting 'but' and the word 'shadows', which recalls the famous Platonic attack on art. We are aware of another side to the argument. And can we accept his implication that one play is more or less as good as another? Because he can generalise, Theseus is an excellent politician, but reactions to art, as to love, require attention to the thing itself, the concrete image before one, as well as to what the thing signifies or the category to which it belongs. One may argue that the situation hardly calls for a considered aesthetic judgement. This is the point exactly. His reaction to the moment is the height of tact, but his remark is somewhat less than the complete statement about art for which it has been taken.

This is why Theseus can dimiss the lovers' story—at the beginning of his long speech about lunatics, lovers and poets—as 'More strange than true'. Here, as elsewhere in Shakespeare's plays, there seems to be an inverse proportion between the vision of the politician and that of the poet. The better one functions as a politician—that is, the more tactfully and rationally one deals with the problems of the everyday world—the less one glimpses of the better 'golden' world which Sidney says is the province of the poet. The politician sees both more and less than the poet: more in the sense that his eye jumps immediately from the concrete object to its category, less in that the generalities he regards are only such as are necessary to make the world work practically. The poet respects the object itself (indeed creates it, in the form of the fable or the image) but sees incarnate in it all the values and meanings of the golden world. His apprehending imagination is like the mind unaffected by the Fall in Marvell's 'The Garden':

> The Mind, that Ocean where each kind
> Does streight its own resemblance find;
> Yet it creates, transcending these,
> Far other Worlds, and other Seas.

But to the politician this is irrelevant to the business at hand. The politician's opinion of the poet is summed up in what Worcester the plotter says after Hotspur's sublime speech on 'bright honour':

> He apprehends a world of figures here,
> And not the form of what he should attend. (I H IV, I. 3)

Theseus rejects the lovers' story since it fits no category except a kind of madness. But even as he speaks we know he is wrong. The story may seem mad. The lovers may be uncertain, when they wake, whether they have been dreaming or awake. But we, the audience, know it happened; it was brought alive for us in the ineradicable image of the action on the stage. But the important point is that we do not know what we know until we have seen Theseus, by contrast, arrive at the wrong conclusion. If one considers his first speech in Act V together with his misunderstanding of what the lovers have been doing when he finds them asleep in the wood, one is faced with a deliberate reduction in his range of view. At the beginning of the play he seems in control of everything—setting the date for his wedding (and thus providing a plausible time-scale within which the drama will take place), coolly deliberating between the opposing forces of Egeus and the younger generation. By the end of Act IV the major events of the play seem to have passed him by. For however adequately his scepticism may respond to the immediate moment, it falls short as an account of what happened.

This is not to say, though, that *A Midsummer Night's Dream* is the story of how Theseus comes to miss the point, or a general satire on politicians. By the end of the play Theseus is not really a character at all; he is a dramatic device used by the author to reinforce the play's main action in the memories of the audience. As Theseus's point of view becomes restricted, so ours expands and becomes firm. William Golding uses the same tactic in *Lord of the Flies*, when he introduces the naval officer at the end of the book. The boys have stripped away every layer of civilisation as they have hunted first pigs, then each other. The officer, in starched whites, sees only a band of scruffy children and assumes they have been playing games. Recalling *The Coral Island*, he thinks British boys should have made some attempt to keep themselves orderly and decent, even on a desert island. As though for reassurance and relief of his embarrassment, he moves his gaze to his 'trim cruiser' anchored in the bay. Like Theseus, the officer ignores both the facts in front of him and their real meaning. He has forgotten—or never realised—what he and his cruiser have in common with the boys' savagery, just as Theseus has forgotten that he too was once a victim of irrational, anarchic romantic love. Both Theseus and the officer are devices for educating the audience or reader. The difference, of course, is that *Lord of the Flies* is hardly a comedy. In the novel the device of the officer forces the reader's attention to a sombre theme of the depravity of fallen man.

When Theseus misunderstands the events in the wood, we are reminded not only of human violence and unreason but of a providential process by which this depravity has been redeemed.

How do the lovers themselves function in Act V? If Theseus considers their story untrue (and thus, indirectly, invites the audience to consider ways in which it *is* true), the lovers simply forget about it. When they wake in the wood, they try desperately to explain to Theseus their feeling that a powerful outside force has been guiding their behaviour. Afterwards they confess to each other that they are not sure what really happened, or whether or not they have been dreaming. This is their moment of greatest honesty and insight: they will not accept easy explanations, and they cannot banish the sense of something bigger than themselves.

Their retreat from even this fragmentary vision, in Act V, is a demand of the comic form: they must reassume the values of their society, and Athens, as its spokesman makes clear at the beginning of Act V, has no place for their story. Yet when they turn from acting in their 'fond pageant' to become the audience at *Pyramus and Thisbe*, we feel a sense of loss. Have they assimilated their experience, or forgotten it? Should not this violent drama of crossed lovers—however absurdly produced—stir in them some memories of their own complaints at being crossed and their own violence?

Instead, taking their cue from Theseus and deriving their witticisms from his, they ridicule the mechanicals. Like Theseus, they are obsessed with categories. Starveling arrives, as 'moon', carrying dog, bush and lantern. Theseus comments:

> This is the greatest error of all the rest; the man should be put into the lantern. How is it else the man i' th' moon?

And a few lines later Demetrius takes up the joke: 'Why, all these should be in the lantern; for all these are in the moon.' This is unfair. The mechanicals may do their best to destroy dramatic illusion (when they go to such lengths to civilise Lion, for instance), but their audience should surely be expected to make the imaginative leap from Starveling's iconography to what it 'presents'. In their concern for categories, the courtiers miss the impact of the concrete image. They also miss its real meaning for them: the moon—even Starveling's presentation of it—should remind them of their own antics by moonlight.

At times the young lovers almost seem to condemn themselves out of their own mouths:

> *Demetrius:* A mote will turn the balance which Pyramus, which Thisbe is the better—he for a man, God warrant us; she for a woman, God bless us.
> *Lysander:* She hath spied him already, with those sweet eyes.

Demetrius thinks of a tiny spot of dust on a scale, but 'mote' was also common usage for a speck in the eye, an association which Lysander unwittingly develops in the next line. The irony is obvious and direct. Demetrius forgets the mote in his own eye which so swayed the balance between his choice of Hermia and Helena.

Theseus and the lovers, then, discount or forget the influence of the supernatural, reinforcing the audience's awareness of it. But Shakespeare provides another comment on what happened in the wood—Bottom's speech when he awakes at the end of Act IV. For all its apparent absurdity we can take it as a direct guide to the significance of the play's action, something which could not be said for even the smoothest of Theseus's assertions. For Bottom is, after all, the very opposite of Theseus. He is the 'bottom' of the hierarchy of which Theseus is the top. Theseus has a prudent regard for categories, whereas Bottom persistently confuses them, as his speech throughout the play makes clear:

> An I may hide my face, let me play Thisbe too.
> I'll speak in a monstrous little voice: 'Thisne, Thisne!' (I. 2)

(as Pyramus)

> I see a voice. Now will I to the chink
> To spy an I can hear my Thisbe's face. . . .
> Will it please you to see the epilogue, or to hear a Bergomask dance between two of our compny? (V. 1)

In terms of Athenian society he is an ass. In the wood he is an ass of another sort. Yet this ass, this 'bottom', is the one character to be granted a vision of the Fairy Queen:

> I have had a most rare vision. I have had a dream past the wit of man to say what dream it was. Man is but an ass if he go about to expound this dream. Methought I was—there is no man can tell what. Methought I was—and methought I had—but man is but a patched fool if he will offer to say what methought I had. The eye of man hath not heard, the ear of man hath not seen, man's hand is not able to taste, his tongue to conceive, nor his heart to report what my dream was! I will get Peter Quince to

> write a ballad of this dream. It shall be called 'Bottom's Dream',
> because it hath no bottom. (IV. I)

This is as different as it could be from Theseus's reactions to the 'dream'.
It is linguistically garbled, whereas his is smoothly delivered. It is not
part of the patter of social discourse, but is announced alone, to no one.
Whereas Theseus, who experienced nothing of the dream, feels qualified
to communicate an opinion on it, Bottom, who saw the Fairy Queen,
communicates nothing.

He does so explicitly (his refusal to comment is the theme of his
speech) and implicitly, by mixing his categories once again. Yet we have
only to translate this from 'Bottom speech' to English (an easy enough
task, since we have been presented with sufficient examples of how he
'scrambles' his language) in order to be reminded of a famous passage
from St. Paul's first Epistle to the Corinthians:

> Things which eye saw not, and ear heard not,
> And *which* entered not into the heart of man,
> Whatsoever things God prepared for them that love him.
>
> (I *Cor.* II. 9)

The 'things' referred to are:

> . . . wisdom among the perfect: yet a wisdom not of this world,
> nor of the rulers of this world, which are coming to nought: . . . God's
> wisdom in a mystery, *even* the *wisdom* that hath been hidden, which
> God foreordained before the worlds unto our glory: which none of
> the rulers of this world knoweth. (I *Cor.* II. 6–8)

Bottom's speech would be 'to the Greeks foolishness' if any of the
influential Athenians were there to hear him. But we laugh too, partly
because he takes so long to tell us that he can tell us nothing, partly at the
way the memories of his 'translation' keep interrupting his flow of
thought. The humour is enriched by the element of parody, not just in
the inversion of the St. Paul passage, but also in the echo of the lovers'
painful attempt to explain their experience to Theseus when they
awake.

Yet we take the speech seriously too. Perhaps Bottom's awkwardness
is, after all, the best expression of the inexpressible. And even through
the indirection of parody, the allusion to St. Paul still works on us. We
know who the ruler of this world is, and can imagine how he will receive
the story the lovers tell. And the stern warning, 'Man is but an ass if he

go about to expound this dream', stays with us throughout the fifth act.

Considered as a single line of action, the scenes from the moment Theseus enters the wood to the end of the play serve to distance the audience—in stages—from the action in the wood. There are several 'plays', of course: the 'fond pageant' itself, the mechanicals' production which is a kind of comment on it, the action which begins when Theseus announces his wedding date and ends when the Athenians leave the stage for bed, and *A Midsummer Night's Dream* itself. Each has its actors and its audience; indeed the main interest in the scenes following the end of the first play (the 'fond pageant') arises when actors become spectators. It is when they watch 'plays' involving other characters than themselves that the mortals run the risk of commenting too facilely on what they are watching, and become asses. From this point of view, Theseus is the greatest ass of all, since although he was an actor long ago in his own pageant of Ariadne and Antiopa, here he remains outside the action of both the wood and the mechanicals' play. The lovers present a kind of truth, however haltingly, about their own experience, but when they watch *Pyramus and Thisbe*, they join Theseus in the smart comments which so make asses of them all. It is as though whatever the similarities between a work of art and our own perceptions of the world, we can never make the imaginative leap between them, never 'streight [our] own resemblance find' in the created image. Is this general rule a theme of the play? Does *A Midsummer Night's Dream* ultimately dismiss the possibility of a valid response to art? Is the audience finally banished as impossible?

I believe the play questions this possibility rather than dismisses it. The question can best be developed through examining briefly the last stage in the process by which the audience is distanced from the wood—the point when the Athenians go to bed and the fairies inherit the stage. If Theseus's point of view were all, or Athens the sum of all wisdom, this (plus or minus an epithalamion) would be the end of the play. Instead, Theseus leaves with what I take to be a figurative, not a literal, reference to fairies: 'Lovers to bed; 'tis almost fairy time'. It does not occur to him that there really are fairies in his palace.

But they come on stage, as though to demonstrate where the power lies. Puck's first words, 'Now the hungry lion roars', remind us that in the real world there are real lions, not the pasteboard creation of the mechanicals. Oberon bestows his blessings by negating (hence reminding us of) the traditional fairy curses:

> Never mole, harelip, nor scar,
> Nor mark prodigious, such as are
> Despisèd in nativity,
> Shall upon their children be.

It is common for the endings of Shakespearean comedies to remind the audience of the everyday world which we are about to re-enter—think of Feste's 'the rain it raineth every day'. But this is more than a device for letting us down gently. It reminds us, by contrast, that for an hour or two we have been immersed in the ideal world of comedy; like Bottom's allusion to St. Paul, it underpins our awareness of the mysterious providential plan which comedy can imitate but which lies beyond the terms of the real world and its rulers. But comedy, because much of its delight is communicated through our aesthetic apprehension of its structure, is not only a form of art, but raises questions about the nature of art as well. The ending of *A Midsummer Night's Dream* reminds us not only of the integrity of the providential action which shapes it, but also of the validity of the golden world. When Puck says:

> If we shadows have offended,
> Think but this, and all is mended:
> That you have but slumbered here
> While these visions did appear.
> And this weak and idle theme,
> No more yielding but a dream, . . .

we take it at first that he dismisses the audience in two ways—sends them home and discounts the possibility that they can respond any more accurately to the play than Theseus did to the lovers' story. But Puck's use of 'shadows', an ironic reflection of Theseus's 'The best in this kind are but shadows', provides substance to a word used only negatively before, as though to say, 'Theseus thinks all elements outside his rational viewpoint to be shadows, but here we are'. Our attention is drawn not to the similarity, but to a potential difference, between our response and Theseus's.

And this is obvious enough, if we think back on Act V. An audience does not have to respond as Theseus does, and later the lovers do. Hippolyta, for example, is a different kind of audience. She believes the lovers' story and will not be put off her belief even by her fiancé's lengthy and plausible assertion that they have been plagued by fantasies. In their discussion which opens Act V, she is allowed the last word, an intelligent —even conclusive—answer to the 'More strange than true' speech:

But all the story of the night told over,
And all their minds transfigured so together,
More witnesseth than fancy's images,
And grows to something of great constancy;
But howsoever, strange and admirable.

This means not only that the lovers all, independently, tell the same story, but that something within her—an instinct, perhaps—prompts her to accept it as true. In other words, she apprehends the resemblance between her experience and the fable, though her feeling of wonder stops her from defining the 'something'.

Shakespeare provides the audience, then, with three responses to the action in the wood. Theseus dismisses the story as a wild flight of fancy —untrue. Hippolyta admits that the story is improbable, but sees a certain consistency in it. Bottom sees it as what Macrobius would call an *oneiros*—that is, an enigmatic dream 'that conceals with strange shapes and veils with ambiguity the true meaning of the information being offered'.[1] We are then invited, indirectly, to apply each of these attitudes to the question of whether *A Midsummer Night's Dream*, or any fiction, is anything more than shadows.

Does any one of these three responses become Shakespeare's 'normative' attitude to fiction? Is Hippolyta's balanced view a model for the audience's approach to the action in the wood and to *A Midsummer Night's Dream*? I think not. It is a mark of the play's inconclusiveness that each of these three views has a certain validity, and that each cancels the other out, to an extent. Even Theseus's doubts about the veracity of the imagination and its works cannot be dismissed as simply wrong. Or rather, one can see his doubts as alternatively 'right' and 'wrong' as one moves further away from the immediate action surrounding his statement. His remarks suit the moment because the audience needs an appropriate sign that the lovers are re-entering the world of reason. Plotted against the action in the wood, his dismissal of the lovers' story is simply wrong, because he says the story is not true, and we know it is. Taken out of context altogether, his statement regains a certain, even profound

[1] Macrobius, *Commentary on the Dream of Scipio*, trans. William Harris Stahl (New York, 1952), p. 90. However, Bottom says only an ass would attempt to 'expound' the dream, whereas Macrobius says the *oneiros* 'requires an interpretation for its understanding' (*ibid.*). I am indebted to Professor Frank Kermode for drawing my attention to Macrobius in this context.

rightness. Even 'The best in this kind are but shadows', although limited, is undeniable, and Puck's 'If we shadows have offended', can be taken not only as an ironic reflection on Theseus's scepticism, but as acknowledgement of an inescapable fact about characters in a work of fiction.

The puzzle over the validity of 'the play' is the greatest in a play containing many puzzles. The characters and what they stand for are ambivalent: the fairies can be taken as benevolent and malevolent; Theseus as powerful in one sense and limited in another; the lovers and the love they invoke as sometimes blind, sometimes enlightened by a redeeming vision. The dangers of the wood—from both without and within the human beings wandering there—are constantly present, and yet they are usually distanced by the formality of the characters and their dialogue. (The exception, when the lovers discard their courtly style to engage in a slanging match and when the violence is allowed to come perilously close to the surface, is by contrast one of the most frightening moments in the play; it is also one of the funniest.)

Is the danger less frightening because it is distanced? or more frightening because so often ignored by the characters and yet so obviously there?

And what about the element of parody in the play? Lying behind it are ghostly echoes of not only 'The Knight's Tale' but that popular medieval genre, the dream vision (we even get, in the wood, a perverted version of the dream-vision garden in *The Parliament of Fowls*, replete with a flower-decked Priapus).[1] In both the *Parliament* and 'The Knight's Tale' the violence of love is distanced by being placed within a formal setting, so that the reader may examine love dispassionately. Does *A Midsummer Night's Dream* gain authority for its treatment of love by 'citing' these distinguished exemplars, or does the subject become trivial because the play pokes fun at the conventions of the romance and the dream vision?

And then, as if these puzzles of tone were not enough, Shakespeare even asks us if plays themselves are anything more than shadows. At the very height of his comic action in *A Midsummer Night's Dream* he

[1] The point is being made only half seriously. However, a decadent example of the dream-vision *genre*, the *Hypnerotomachia Poliphili* (Venice, 1499), includes a scene in which an ass covered with flowers is sacrificed by nymphs before the altar of Priapus. The description is accompanied by a woodcut. Sir Robert Dallington published a shortened translation in London (*The Strife of Love in a Dreame*, 1592), but he cut out both text and illustration of the altar-of-Priapus episode.

can entertain doubts about the validity of that action. He even doubts the medium through which those doubts are expressed.

The puzzles thicken at the end of the play as the audience is withdrawn from the central action. Attempt to solve the puzzles, and you become the ass that Bottom said you would become. You also miss the play's real impact, because it should be obvious by now that Shakespeare uses complexity—or the illusion of complexity—as a dramatic device. You are supposed to remain puzzled, until finally the various 'intellectual' responses to the play (and the play within the play, and the play within that) cancel each other out and force you to look elsewhere for comfort. The real meaning of *A Midsummer Night's Dream* is that no one 'meaning' can be extracted from the puzzles with which a fiction presents its audience. We must share what Keats called Shakespeare's '*Negative Capability*':

> . . . that is when man is capable of being in uncertainties, Mysteries, doubts, without any irritable reaching after fact and reason.[1]

And then when the clash of dilemmas dies away, we may recall our *experience* of the action in the wood, and of the play itself; we may remember that we apprehended—even if we did not comprehend (or comprehend how we apprehended)—a certain 'local habitation and a name' called *A Midsummer Night's Dream*.

[1] Letter to George and Thomas Keats, 21 December 1817, in *The Letters of John Keats*, ed. Maurice Buxton Forman (Oxford, 1952), p. 71.

Select Bibliography

Quotations from *A Midsummer Night's Dream* are from the New Penguin Shakespeare edition, which is now perhaps the most convenient and useful text for student use in this country. Quotations from other Shakespeare plays come from the one-volume Oxford text, and the Chaucer references are taken from F. N. Robinson's second edition.

Suggestions for further reading

C. L. Barber, *Shakespeare's Festive Comedy*, Princeton, 1959.

K. M. Briggs, *The Anatomy of Puck*, London, 1959.

John Russell Brown, *Shakespeare and his Comedies*, London, 1957.

Wolfgang Clemen, Introduction to the Signet Classic edition of *A Midsummer Night's Dream*, New York, 1963.

G. K. Hunter, *Shakespeare: the Late Comedies* (British Council Writers-and-their-Work Series), London, 1962.

Frank Kermode, 'The Mature Comedies' (*Stratford-upon-Avon Studies III: The Early Shakespeare*), London, 1961.

Kenneth Muir, *Shakespeare's Sources* (Vol. 1), London, 1957.

Howard Nemerov, 'The Marriage of Theseus and Hippolyta', *Kenyon Review* XVIII (1956).

Paul Olsen, '*A Midsummer Night's Dream* and the meaning of Court Marriage', *ELH* XXIV (1955).

David Young, *Something of Great Constancy*, Yale, 1966.

Index